THE HETEROSEXUAL
MANIFESTO

THE HETEROSEXUAL MANIFESTO

An Avant-Garde Syllogistic Treatise Confronting The Ineffable

Why The World Is Currently A Dystopia, How It Got To Be That Way
And What, If Anything, Can Be Done About It

Princess Eroica

To order additional copies of this book, contact:
Xlibris Corporation
1-888-795-4274
www.Xlibris.com
Orders@Xlibris.com
35925

Contents

Dedicated To Dr. Evelyn Hooker For Her Pioneering And Invaluable Scientific Work That Literally Forced The American Psychiatric Association, In 1973, To Remove Homosexuality From the Diagnostic And Statistical Manuel Of Mental Disorders

And

Dedicated To Isaac Newton For Writing
Philosophiæ Naturalis Principia Mathematica

And

Dedicated To My Dear Friend Q For Being Brawn, Brains, And Beauty

About The Author Princess Eroica

In Honor Of Samuel Langhorne Clemens For Being Mark Twain

"What the hell is a *nom de guerre*? Who the hell is Princess Eroica (and, more importantly, why the hell should I care)? I thought this book was written by Vincent A. Clemmons. I'm disoriented and confused. What the hell is going on here?!"

The phrase *nom de guerre* is French and roughly translates into *war name*; meaning, it's an "assumed name" under which one goes to clandestine war and conducts surreptitious activities. It's kind of like a fancy-schmancy *nom de plume* or pseudonym for terrorists, whether they be crazed religious jihadists determined to bring about a totalitarian theocracy strictly by means of violence or civil civil-libertarians determined to bring about human freedom strictly by means of non-violence. (I like to think that I am in the latter camp, lol.) Anyway, having long ago publicly declared *non-violent* war against *Heterosexual Supremacy*, Princess Eroica is the *war name* that I, Vincent Aubrey Clemmons, took. Vincent Aubrey Clemmons is the person who wrote this book, *The Heterosexual Manifesto*; Princess Eroica is the *alter-ego* name under which this book, *The Heterosexual Manifesto*, is published. I hope that cleared things up for you.

Now, you are probably asking why the name Princess Eroica. (Why not something a little more masculine or pithy or droll or gangsta or hardcore or whatever.) Well, for those in the know, *Eroica* is the title of Ludwig van Beethoven's third symphony (in E flat major). Beethoven had originally conceived of dedicating his third symphony to Napoleon Bonaparte, because Beethoven greatly admired the ideals of the *French Revolution* and thought that Napoleon embodied those ideals; thus, he titled his third symphony *Eroica* (Italian, meaning heroic) in honor of Napoleon. However, when Napoleon later showed himself to be nothing more than just another thug, despot and megalomaniac, by declaring himself *Emperor of the French*, it is said that Beethoven become sickened and disgusted and went to the table where his completed third symphony lay and took hold of the title-page and scratched the name Bonaparte out so violently with a knife he created a hole in the paper—and immediately, Beethoven changed the title of his third symphony to *Sonifonia eroica, composta per festeggiare il sovvenire d'un grand'uomo*, Heroic symphony, composed to celebrate the memory of a great man. (Nevertheless, Beethoven, having learned later in life that to err is human, to forgive is divine, wrote to his publisher in the summer of 1804 that "The title of the symphony is really *Bonaparte*.) Anyway, to make a long story short, the word *Eroica* has a very long and storied provenance dealing with heroism, and more specifically with the French Revolution's ideals of *liberté, egalité*, and *fraternité*, and that is why I chose it as part of my *nom de guerre*. I also chose the word Eroica because most English speakers have a terrible time enunciating it and inherently make the *Freudian Slip* of pronouncing it *Erotica*. (I guess I am a semantic prankster at heart and just like to trip people up every now and then.) Even my own dear, learned mother mistakenly pronounces it Erotica.

I chose the word Princess to go in front of the word *Eroica* as an homage to H.R.H. Princess Diana of Wales, simply because I believe she showed *sui generis* personal grit and grace under pressure by standing up to the imposing House of Windsor and the omnipotent Queen of England. I did not choose the word Princess to go in front of the word *Eroica* because I think I am a Princess or because I want to be a Princess, or because I want to be treated like a Princess; I do not live vicariously as a female or live vicariously through females, and I do not want to be a female or to be treated like a female—the way *some* gay men do. (I am both the antithesis of a royalist and the antithesis of a "big ole' queen.") I would have chosen the word Prince to go in front of the word Eroica, but there currently is no Prince that I greatly respect and admire. (Where's my prince charming, indeed.) Aren't the boys suppose to be the ballsy ones?

So, there you have it and now you know who exactly wrote this book, *The Heterosexual Manifesto*; what a *nom de guerre* is, why Eroica and why Princess. To learn more about the author, Vincent A. Clemmons, a.k.a. Princess Eroica, please visit:

www.VincentClemmons.com

Warning! Warning!

Aperçu

In Honor Of Thomas Paine For Writing *The Age Of Reason*

fiat justitia, ruat cælum

This work is not child's play; it was not written for children nor was it written for adults who think like children. So, if you've built your world around self-delusion (better known as *infallibility*), perhaps you should be reading the Bible, the Qur'an, the Tanakh etcetera.

I am a *Heresiarch* and, out of conscience, I consider it my duty as a citizen of planet earth to think the unthinkable and speak the unspeakable for the express purpose of **problem prevention and problem solving**—better known as change, which is the only constant. As a scientific humanist, freethinking philosopher, experimental intellectual and flexible deist, let me forewarn you that my dialectical musings are most likely greatly unsettling to anyone who is not *self-actualized*. (And may be terribly distressing even to anyone who is *self-actualized*!) Being that I am an ardent believer and practitioner of *fallibilism*, you may find my motto "I don't know what I don't know" very disconcerting. Indeed, because we live in a world that is an *ochlocratic* Plutocracy (mob rule by the wealthy), my dissentingly heuristic ruminations are almost virtually guaranteed to be at odds with your most basic *enculturation*; and thus, likely to make you go apoplectic. If you have not at the very least read *Your Erroneous Zones*, *Pulling Your Own Strings* and, the *magnum opus*, *The Sky's The Limit*, respectively, all by the indispensable Dr. Wayne W. Dyer, I beg you, read no further.

Because, as a *Heresiarch*, I am axiomatically going to appeal to your prurient interests, whatever your contemporary community standards, and I am axiomatically going to fulfill the other two prongs of the *Miller Test*, **this work is, technically, obscene and thus, technically, banned by definition of the U.S. Supreme Court.** (Although this work is figuratively, not literally, banned, it's still something you should know, before you continue your little reading misadventure.) And with that, I humbly submit for your reading displeasure the ultimate creative non-fiction literary *magnum opus;* it is inarguably the most scientific, the most rigorous, the most impartial, and the most dispassionate creative non-fiction literary work ever written—and, precisely because of that, it is the most fearless, the most brutal, the most daunting, the most disturbing, the most incendiary, the most polarizing, the most divisive, the most traumatizing, and the most dangerous creative non-fiction literary work ever written.

No prisoners will be taken.
Lasciate ogne speranza, voi ch'intrate.

F.Y.I.

All Of The Authors And Books Below Are Currently, Technically, Banned
By The U.S. Supreme Court:

My Favorite Banned Straight Fiction Straight Author:

Theodore Seuss Geisel, a.k.a. Dr. Sueuss, for Writing

How The Grinch Stole Christmas

My Favorite Banned Straight Fiction Book:

Adventures Of Huckleberry Finn by Samuel L. Clemens, a.k.a. Mark Twain

---

My Favorite Banned Non-Fiction Straight Author:

Dr. Wayne W. Dyer For Writing *Your Erroneous Zones*

My Favorite Banned Non-Fiction Book:

The Sky's The Limit by Dr. Wayne W. Dyer

My Favorite Banned Gay Poet:

Walt Whitman For Writing *Leaves Of Grass*

My Favorite Banned Gay Book of Poetry:

Leaves of Grass by Walt Whitman

My Favorite Banned Gay Playwright:

Tennessee Williams For Writing *Suddenly Last Summer*

My Favorite Banned Gay Play:

The Children's Hour by Lillian Hellman

My Favorite Banned Gay Fiction Gay Author:

Charles Nelson for writing *The Boy Who Picked The Bullets Up*

My Favorite Banned Gay Fiction Book:

The Boy Who Picked The Bullets Up by Charles Nelson

My Favorite Banned Gay Non-Fiction Gay Author:

Michel Foucault for writing *The History of Sexuality*

My Favorite Banned Gay Non-Fiction Book:

The History of Sexuality by Michel Foucault

Reading Instructions For
The Heterosexual Manifesto

(Especially For The Exacting And The Persnickety)

Dedicated To Eric Arthur Blair, a.k.a. George Orwell, For Writing *1984*
The Greatest Work Of Non-Fiction Mistaken For Fiction

Understanding The Nexus-Power-Levers Politics,
Law, Religion & Medicine
Is Key To Comprehending *The Heterosexual Manifesto*

> Who controls the past controls the future.
> Who controls the present controls the past.
> —George Orwell

To better help quickly familiarize you with the intellectual tour de force that is *The Heterosexual Manifesto*, please take note.

First and foremost, you should understand all my written work is resistance writing and resistance literature, underground writing and underground literature in the vane of George Orwell; and I make no bones about it. This treatise, *The Heterosexual Manifesto*, is no different from any of my previous written work, except in that it is purposefully extremely unpleasant and hard to swallow. It is not some highfalutin altruistic or idealistic work that attempts to influence people; it is a grand and noxious polemic designed to give everyone (and I do mean everyone) serious heartburn. It is not some light or airy or, dare I say, gay piece of writing; it is a heavy, dense and extremely rigorous conjecture.

This particular work is an extremely heretical *academic work of dada art* that vainly attempts to explain why humanity is currently in the mess that it is in; that is, indeed, if you believe humanity is in any mess at all. It is a radically *counter-counter-counterculture*, groundbreaking, and vanguard work that is purposely contrarian to that which is held sacred by all and sundry, save one; and therefore is axiomatically misanthropic, if not necessarily nihilistic, and therefore verboten—at least by definition of the powers that be. (Advocating the rape and murder of children pales in comparison to this writing, I am afraid to say.) And speaking of the powers that be, how often have the powers that be proven to be the powers that aught not be? The list is endless, of course, but, not surprisingly, Hitler and Pol Pot immediately spring to mind.

Manipulating the nexus-power-levers Politics, Law, Religion and Medicine made both Hitler and Pol Pot possible, and it has made countless other totalitarian and authoritarian con artists possible. **This stringent, landmark, revolutionary and, indeed, front line work says that totalitarian and authoritarian manipulation of the human species, which has wrought nothing but indescribable horror, is only possible by way of pseudoscience masquerading as real science; in our case, a pseudoscience I have christened *Scientific Heterosexism*.** This pseudoscience, *Scientific Heterosexism*, is a strange amalgam of anti-intellectual toxic brews that is systemic and systematic, encapsulating all pseudosciences, unlike for example, say, *Scientific Racism*, which is merely haphazardly irrational and maudlin. (Where's *Scientific Racism* says that I, a person of Jewish and African descent, was put on this earth for the sole purpose of being a slave to a White/Caucasian; *Scientific Heterosexism* says that I, a homosexual male, was not put on this earth at all. Essentially, *Scientific Heterosexism* says that you are not reading this work, because I do not exist, because I was never born to be able to write it.) The pseudoscience *Scientific Heterosexism*, it all seems so tantalizingly amusing—that is, if it all weren't so deadly, deadly *bathetic*.

More all-encompassing than *Scientific Racism*, and a trillion times more pernicious, *Scientific Heterosexism* is a totalitarian and authoritarian pseudoscience that, like all illogic, is built upon a foundation of presuppositions, presumptions, and assumptions to form premises—when logic dictates that absolutely nothing can be presupposed, presumed and assumed; **that before a premise is a premise, a premise must be proven fact or all that follows the premise is inherently illogical.** The presuppositions, presumptions, and assumptions that form pseudoscience's premises usually or almost always get their validity or bona fides from long history or so-called religion (voodoo), mythology (half-truths), and/or from custom (habit); i.e. some ancient ritual or cultural practice has supposedly *stood the test of time*—as an aside, isn't it ironic that my and your eventual death has managed to stand the test of time. Anyway, manipulating the nexus-power-levers Politics, Law, Religion, and Medicine to make the world in your exact spitting image (the very definition of narcissism) is easy when pseudoscience, masquerading as real science, is on your side. How, you ask, does using pseudoscience to control the nexus-power levers Politics, Law, Religion, and Medicine work. Well, in case you haven't noticed, the nexus-power-levers Politics, Law, Religion, and Medicine give *legal cover* for all manner of VIOLENCE to forcefully impose your will and, literally and physically, make the world in your exact spitting image. Legal cover for violent and Machiavellian means and ends is always necessary, and relying on pseudoscience to manipulate the nexus-power-levers Politics, Law, Religion, and Medicine inherently provide such legal cover.

What are my personal favorites, you ask, of pseudoscience, masquerading as real science, manipulating the nexus-power-levers Politics, Law, Religion, and Medicine to achieve such diabolical results as described above. Well, my personal favorites: *Drapetomania* and *Dysaethesia Aethiopica*. For me, these two pseudoscience doozies exemplify the manipulation of the nexus-power-levers Politics, Law, Religion, and Medicine to wreck indefinable havoc and agony on countless lives for countless years. (Unfortunately, the excuse that **we as humans simply didn't know any better** is not an excuse at all; it's just a fancy way of saying that, when it comes to *pure science*, we as a human species are the exact opposite of rigorous, painstaking, introspective, and questioning—or, in other words, when it comes to *pure science*, we as a human species are lazy, indolent, trifling hoes.) If you are not afflicted with, or even aware of, *Drapetomania* or *Dysaethesia Aethiopica*, two phantasm psychiatric maladies that are a direct result of pseudoscience, thank your lucky stars. All I can say is Samuel A. Cartwright, M.D., makes Joseph Mengele, M.D., look like Quincy, M.D., and that's no joke. (The medical profession may have its Hippocratic Oath, but after familiarizing yourself with the infamous malpractice of Samuel Adolphus Cartwright, M.D., and some of his contemporaries in the medical field, you may think it should be spelled the *Hypocratic* Oath.) Time may heal all of humanity's wounds, but I hope you'll agree that it is best if so-called medical doctors are not the ones inflicting the wounds upon humanity in the first place.

Anyway, the history of so-called psychiatry and medicine (and, thus, the history of human civilization itself) is replete with mistake after egregious mistake, regardless how inadvertent or well-intentioned, of what is supposedly normal behavior juxtaposed to what is supposedly abnormal behavior; what behavior is supposedly good for humanity and what behavior is supposedly bad for humanity. In the end, of course, whoever wins gets to control the nexus-power-levers of Politics, Law, Religion, and Medicine to define what and who is normal and what and who is abnormal; what and who is good for humanity, what and who is bad for humanity, etcetera—and, conversely, whoever loses must live with the definitions, set by the winner, of what and who is normal and what and who is abnormal, whether the loser likes it or not. With the axiomatic axiom "might makes right" understood, the only question is are you on the losing end of the nexus-powers-levers Politics, Law, Religion and Medicine, or are you on the winning end of the nexus-powers-levers Politics, Law, Religion and Medicine? *Alexander The Great* understood the question very well, and it is why he exist, while those he conquered do not exist: *Naqoyqatsi*—and winner takes all.

Nota Bene:

> Men imagine that their minds have the command of language, but it
> often happens that language bears rule over their minds.
>   —Francis Bacon

Now, some grammatical grace notes. This is *creative non-fiction*, literally, on the cutting edge. Remember, this being a radical, innovatory, controversial, and dissenting expository work of art, standard conventions of current English composition, pronunciation, spelling, style, and punctuation are null and void; thus, discombobulating syntax in this lucubration is a *fait accompli*. Grammar-wise, if something in this incendiary, irreverent, indecent, pioneering, and profane tract seems even slightly askew or amiss, no matter how innocuous, keep in mind, it was written precisely to be that way. (You may notice that some *homonyms* and *homographs* are characteristically inverted, oftentimes on purpose and other times by sheer serendipity.) This being a nervy and highly *experimental scientific art work*, I reserve the right to be not only politically incorrect but also to be grammatically incorrect; this work is dada thought, dada philosophy, dada science and dada literature—so, any solecism in my oeuvre, even if consciously inadvertent and unintentional, is inherently *grammatical parapraxis*. And if you think this is some lame attempt on my part to excuse or cover-up the fact that I am a lousy grammarian (who, sheepishly, wouldn't know a *dangling participle* if it bit me on my dangling dick) and some lame effort on my part to cover my grammatical ass, you are absolutely right. *MUTATIS MUTANDIS*

Avant-Propos

In honor of Socrates for being a studious gadfly and intellectual martyr; and for supposedly "corrupting the morals" of ancient Athen's youths.

Angels Rush In Where Fools Fear To Tread

Who Am I?
I Am Your Worse Nightmare;
I Am A Faggot Who Knows What It's All About
                                        —Princess Eroica

I am not a politician, I am a provocateur. It is not my job to please or placate you, it is my job to upset and disturb you. It is not my job to tell you things you want to hear, it is my job to tell you things you don't want to hear. It is not my job to feed your delusions, it is my job to deconstruct your illusions. It is not my job to be your friend, it is my job to be your enemy. It is not my job to so-call "share your values," it is my job to mock your values. It is not my job to be *persona grata*, it is my job to be *persona non grata*—it is particularly my job to be *persona non grata* to so-called gays, lesbians, bisexuals, and transgenders. (And if I did not do my job, you would say, "Oh, look, there's another lazy Black person." And if I did not do my job well, you would say, "Oh, look, there's another 'incompetent' Black person." And if I did not do my job and do it well, you would say, "Oh, look there's another 'lazy and incompetent' Black person." Or, since I am a homosexual male, you would say, "Oh, look, there's another craven fag, without the balls, strength and courage to do a thoroughly difficult, unpleasant task that must get done." Or, you would say . . . Well, suffice it, if I did not do my job and do it well, the list of what you would say is virtually *ad infinitum*, since my being Black and being a fag in our Orwellian heterosexist society gives you *impoetic* license to damn me if I do do my job and *impoetic* license to damn me if I do not do my job. Being Black and being a fag, I am eternally in a lose lose situation with the likes of 99.9% of the human population.) True, no good deed goes unpunished, and I am sure I will be crucified in my lifetime for bothering to write this tract; but just think what they would say about me if I didn't bother to write this tract.

I am a worker bee, not a queen bee, and my job is essentially to be humanity's inverse court jester. As far as my writing is concerned, no one person and no one group is beyond reproach and nothing is taboo. No question is off limits, because it is only through unlimited questioning can problem prevention and problem solving be brought to fruition, and problem prevention and problem solving are both the means and the end of life itself. That said, the politically correct right and the politically correct left (especially the outrageously politically correct so-called gays, lesbians, bisexuals and transgenders) are anathema as far as I am concerned and a direct threat to humanity itself, because they try to stifle the only constant, which is change = problem prevention and problem solving. Therefore, in my writings, I am forever trying to perfect the art of the politically incorrect, and especially trying to perfect the art of the politically incorrect as far as the so-called gays, lesbians, bisexuals and transgenders are concerned. (Of course, I would rather be despised by all so-called gays, lesbians, bisexuals and transgenders, rather than be loved by even one so-called straight person.) This is my daunting, thankless job; to upset the applecart (especially the applecart of the sexual status quo, of which so-called gays, lesbians, bisexuals and transgenders dutifully play their part). It's not a pretty picture. So, perhaps you had better quit while you are ahead?

My last two books of *avant-garde prose poetry confronting the ineffable*, *Advocatus Diaboli* and *Caveat Emptor*, were purposely and stridently written to be politically incorrect, but in all honesty I don't know if they actually were politically incorrect, even if that was my grasping intent. Upon much closer introspection, even if my previous work is considered incendiary by whomever, I now realize I was unconsciously holding back because I was consciously playing by the rules set by the status quo, namely heterosexuals. And, in the inadvertent process of being so harmonious, I unintentionally played right into the hands of *the powers that be* (better known as heterosexuals) by coming across as the stereotypical weak and mincing homosexual male. Well, *humanum est errare*. I ask your forgiveness; this book, *The Heterosexual Manifesto*, is my atonement, and I will not be "mincing" any words this time around.

With this work, *The Heterosexual Manifesto*, I question the supremacy of heterosexuality, and (because heterosexuality is mistakenly considered indispensable for the survival of the human race) simply by questioning the supremacy of heterosexuality, I will, hopefully, be labeled a *misanthrope*—hope springs eternal! (I can only pray this purposely obscene work will become #1 on the *Index Librorum Prohibitorum* or, at least, the #1 blockbuster worst-seller on the New York Times' Bestseller list.) And with that, in this writing, all bridges are burned; no one person or one group is spared and no one person or one group comes away unscathed; and I, happily, come away smelling like a skunk, since I am burdened with far too many friends and in desperate need of enemies. In short, *The Heterosexual Manifesto* will leave all and sundry gasping for air, because it is my job, however unappreciated, to be an *equal opportunity offender*. Absolutely no one will be spared my grim reaping. This scorched earth, take no prisoners writing is necessitated by the fact that, in all of human history, the supremacy of heterosexuality has never before been questioned—until now, that is. Because the supremacy of heterosexuality is mistakenly considered *axiomatic* (self-evident), and indeed even considered sacred and profound (which is hilarious to me), the supremacy of heterosexuality has effectively escaped all critique and dissection. Well, no more. Being the first person to ever question the legitimacy and supremacy of heterosexuality is pretty heady stuff, but I think I am up to the challenge. And, as for my being a *misanthrope* (or just a kindly ole' curmudgeon, *sans* Andy Rooney), well, the human race has survived plagues, epidemics, pandemics, Idi Amin, Khmer Rouge Rouge and Pink Flamingos, so I think it will survive my musings—not to mention the fact, it all depends on who is defining the word *misanthrope* (and that primarily depends on who has the most money). We all have a cross to bare; mine is this work, *The Heterosexual Manifesto*, deconstructing the supremacy of heterosexuality.

Now that you know what the book is about, I only say that you should be mentally and emotionally forewarned; though this vexing work, *The Heterosexual Manifesto*, is avant-garde dialects, it is still never-the-less dialectics—and, for good measure, in the disadvantageous vein of Charles Darwin's endlessly controversial Theory of Evolution. (This is in many ways a *mathematical literary work* and a *literary mathematical work*. So, it is not exactly easy-reading—note that the cogent complexity, pedagogic severity, and cerebral intensity of this particular work, *The Heterosexual Manifesto*, is indicated by the fact that it is published under my *nom de guerre*.) And what is it exactly that makes this innovatory composition, *The Heterosexual Manifesto*, so academically hard? In short, what I am saying in this sweeping discourse is that, if the human race is to survive, the sexual *status quo* must be upended—and that the clock is ticking. Understand, because the very basis of this world-shattering, mind-boggling book is purposely designed to tear asunder your most basic *enculturation*, you are not going to like this work (in fact, you will hate it), and it is all the more reason why I earnestly and strenuously urge you not to read it. However, should you be so bold and

bodacious to proceed, appreciate that this futuristic work, *The Heterosexual*
Manifesto, **is not for the rationally indolent, craven or challenged; intellectually,**
I am going where no man or woman has gone before. Doctrinaires, buckle up,
because it is going to be a bumpy ride—your didactic buttons will be pushed
and your scholastic nerves will be plucked. Guaranteed. If you subscribe to
"political correctness," whether on the right, left or in the middle, this is a
nightmare piece of work and to be avoided at all cost.

As for my supposed "incorrect" polemics, well, when a ne'er-do-well buffoon
and megalomaniac like George W. Bush can outrageously steal a U.S. presidential
election via a racist Electoral College System, via an even more racist U.S. Supreme
Court, that's when you know *politics* is not the elixir but the cause and effect
of all that ails. Popularity contests, better known as politics, whether correct or
incorrect—depending on who is defining politics, and correct and incorrect—is
not the solution; politics, popularity contests, is/are the problem. In other words,
what I am saying to you is this, "I don't need your fucking stamp of approval!"

Needless to say, all depending on whose ox is being gored, this work is not so
much incendiary or vitriolic as it is downright toxic, and purposely so. Imbeciles,
and those without a sense of humor or a sense of impropriety, will probably label
this, *The Heterosexual Manifesto*, my third major work, so-called "hate speech."
Well, *chacun ses gouts, c'est la vie*! I like to think of this particular work as a kind of
inverse *Mein Kampf* for the well read, heterosexist, Aryan jet-set. Being an avowed
Heresiarch, this particularly multifarious and troubling work, *The Heterosexual*
Manifesto, is designed to disjoint, dismay, traumatize, disgust, and infuriate, but
ultimately to enlighten you. In fact, if you, after having read *The Heterosexual*
Manifesto, are not completely exasperated, distraught and in a state of utter despair,
then I will deem this particular work an absolute, unqualified, abject failure. (No
literary pain, no intellectual gain, if you will.) The rationale of all this *sturm und*
drang on my part is quite simply to crush the reader, forcing him or her to reach such
a state of shock, rage and despondency that he or she has an epiphany of cathartic
proportions; eventually leading to a rethinking of all that the reader knows or has
ever known *for the express purpose of problem prevention and problem solving*.

Despite all my best efforts at aggravation, in the end, this is what is commonly
referred to sneeringly and snarlingly by the *hoi polloi* as a moot (read: academic)
work; meaning it is supposedly written by an "effete snob who characterizes himself
as an intellectual," as the great thirty-ninth Vice-President of the United States,
Spiro Agnew, put it. Well, I guess you can't please all the people all the time or
even some of the people some of the time. *Trahison des clercs?* Perhaps. I am a
mad literary scientist and these are my perilous philological experiments; I am a
coquettish literary terrorist and these are my scholarly ticking time bombs; I am

a revolutionary literary satirist and these are my bluest of black comedies; I am a fanatical literary confectioner and these are my sickly-sweet intellectual bonbons. All that understood, as a cosmically mocking aside, isn't it sardonic that Jesus Christ was a heretic and that that is the very reason he was crucified upon the cross? (Not that I would ever compare myself to Jesus Christ, of course, LOL.) With this diabolical writing, as with Jesus' heterodox crucifixion for being unorthodox, I prove once and for all that life is truly stranger than fiction.

So, there you have it. Those in the know know, and now you know. I am not the average, clueless tacky queen that compromises 99.9% of the homosexual male population. (Are you getting that sinking feeling yet?) I am the faggot your mother never warned you about, because she didn't think such an exquisite and feral creature existed or she didn't think such a brave, ferocious and fearless creature ever could exist. I am the faggot, the only faggot, courageous enough to stand up to the forces of evil, better known as heterosexuals, and their sycophant enablers, better known as so-called gays, lesbians, bisexuals and transgenders. I am the first and only human to ever question heterosexuality, homosexuality et al. So let it be written, so let it be done.

A Special Note:

About My Supposed "Reclaiming" Of The F Word
Dedicated To Harvey Milk For Literally Standing Up To The Powers That Be

---

> The only motive that guided me was my ardent love of my people.
>
> —Herman Goering

What can I say? This being my most subversive, no-holds-barred work to date, I simply could not write *The Heterosexual Manifesto* without setting the epithet FAGGOT ablaze, as if it were a Molotov cocktail, and hurling it at every chance I got. The soubriquet FAGGOT is a pejorative *synonym* (not a *euphemism*) for the words: coward, pusillanimous, spineless, fearful, gutless, pathetic, craven, weak, timorous etc., as opposed to the *antonyms* of all the aforementioned words (which, of course, need not be listed here, since we all know what those words are). Like the N word, the F word is a thoroughly troublesome word that has had a long and strange career. (Too long and way too strange for me to detail here and now, but rest assured, the word FAGGOT is, or at one time has been, haphazardly and variously defined in the Oxford English Dictionary (O.E.D.)—the mother of all English dictionaries and thesauri, and the standard by which all other English dictionaries and thesauri are measured—as: "a bundle of sticks," as "a kind of meatball," as "a cigarette," as "an old or unpleasant woman," as "a man hired into military service to fill out the ranks at muster" and so on. Obviously, the differences defining the world FAGGOT in *British English* versus *American English* become all too apparent and sometimes muddy the waters of just what exactly FAGGOT means now and what it has meant in the past.) As you already know, the word is most often thrown at boys or men who don't meet someone else's high standards of how a boy or man should act; as in, with enough masculinity, bravery, toughness, steadfastness, courage, balls et al, however you want to put it. My use of the word is not suppose to shock so much as it is suppose to dull or bore. Eventually, we become desensitized to whatever is constantly being thrown our way; so it's only natural you'll soon not even notice when I use the word FAGGOT." This desensitizing takes away the power of the word to hurt through its slashing abruptness, since the word does not simply become familiar, but it becomes downright common and lackluster. (Frankly, I don't know if what I just wrote above is being facetious or satirical or sardonic, but I like it anyway.) Let the hurling of the word FAGGOT begin in earnest!

An Even More Special Note:

About How The Politically Correct Right, Left, And Center Have Literally And Figuratively Hijacked The Intellectual Concepts *Existentialism* and *Relativism* By & For Illogical Means And By & For Illogical Ends

Dedicated To *Galileo Galilei*
For Literally Laying His Life On The Line For The Mathematics Of Physics

---

I am free of all prejudice; I hate everyone equally.

—W.C. Fields

As of late, having a Ph.D. in Philosophy has gotten a bum rap and who can honestly argue why. (Ph.D in Philosophy, meaning a "Doctor of Philosophy of Philosophy." As opposed to, say, a Ph.D. in Physics, meaning a "Doctor of Philosophy of Physics." Anyway, you get the picture with these highfalutin academic titles and ephemera.) Poor Nietzche (as in Friedrich), poor Kierkegaard (as in Soren), poor Heidegger (as in Martin), poor Jaspers (as in Karl) and last, but certainly not least, poor Sartre (as in Jean-Paul). None of them, they never saw the demonization of philosophy coming, and certainly did not foresee the demonization of *intellectualism* per se coming. (Which only proves there is, indeed, an actual Ivory Tower. Where? Somewhere.) All the good intentioned thinking by these philosopher kings to get humanity out of the mess known as entropy and randomness, caused by "abstraction," has seemingly only landed humanity in even more entropy and randomness, caused by "abstraction." (Which only proves that the road to Hell is, indeed, paved with good intentions. How? Somehow.) Regardless, let me state unequivocally that these philosophers are not the culprits for the politically correct right, left and center having taken their ideas and twisted and warped them for *illogical means and illogical ends*. But, just how did we get to a place where gangsta rappers proclaim, "It's all good,' and no one ever actually takes them to task for such intellectually indefensible thinking!? Well, let me state, again unequivocally, "It is *not* all good!" Call me a so-called "elitist," call me a "snob," call me "high-and-mighty," call me "snooty," call me an "uppity nigger," call me a "size queen," call me "the devil incarnate," but there simply have to be some standards! (Just because Hitler, Mussolini et al insisted on remaking the world in their own "supremacist" image, does not mean humanity shouldn't ask difficult and inevitably unpleasant questions, and then determine that some things are "logical" and some things are "illogical." Or, at least for the expressed purpose of *problem prevention and problem solving*, come to a determination that some things are "productive" and some things are "counterproductive," especially when it comes to preventing pain and solving pain.) We have all become so "prickly," "touchy" and "overly-sensitive" because of some humans' incalculable narcissism and because of some of humanity's worse excesses, that setting any kind of "standards" or putting up any "limits" or making any "distinctions" of any kind has become almost anathema. This is extremely dangerous!—Suddenly, all the fascists-cloaked-as-conservatives (better known as crypto-fascists) who have excoriated me in the past, their ears start to perk up in agreement.—I am not advocating a world of so-called "absolutes" (moral, ethical or otherwise) or even a world of so-called "universalisms," (moral, ethical or otherwise) as some who want to remake the world in their own spitting image do (the crazed Islamic Theocrats in Iran and Saudi Arabia immediately come to mind), but I am saying there is such a thing as *relativism in thought*, which, though amorphous, is both real and surreal, and there is a misnomer *physical relativism*—which is a human delusion *borne* of faulty reasoning, but primarily *borne* of wishful thinking. (By the way, you should know that Einstein's *General Theory of Relativity* and his *Special Theory of Relativity*, both dealing with quantum mechanics, and the philosophical concept of *Relativism*, dealing with intellectual dialectics, are ironically and inextricably linked yet wholly incongruent; but we'll save all that hullabaloo for another time and another place.) Human beings have done a lot of things to make you not so proud to be a human, so it is understandable that a person may descend into a state of psychosis about the physicality of life itself. Well, wishful thinking, which is just a fancy phrase for "escapist thinking," is like trying to run from your own shadow; it's futile. The politically correct right, left and center resort to "escapist thinking," in the form of *physical relativism*, to try to get away from the harsh and cruel physical reality that we all live in and that simply will not go away (that is, that will not go away until the day we die; and, of course, death is another harsh physical reality some people would rather "escape" from—but then, I could go on *ad infinitum* about all the harsh physical realities we as humans must face up to but refuse to). This "escapist thinking," in the form of *physical relativism*, is extremely treacherous; just as any drug addict who takes a drug to *temporarily* "escape" his or her problems knows—note that the emphasis is on the word temporary, since the problem that the drug addict is trying to "escape" is never really gone, which becomes all too apparent to the drug addict once the "high" has worn off, causing yet another problem, namely addiction to the "high" to temporarily "escape," compounding an already bad situation by making it much worse, thereby instigating a "vicious cycle" of "high" followed by a even more devastating "low," requiring and even greater "high" the next time *ad infinitum*. (By now you're probably a little sick of me using the Latin *ad infinitum*, but it's the best way to describe certain situations.) Needless to say, I could go on *ad infinitum* about the inherent illogic of the politically correct right, left and center, but that would be as futile as **me** trying to run from my own shadow. That understood, suffice it to say, this is a purposely and thoroughly blasphemous work intended to make everyone, and I do mean everyone, cry foul; so, the politically correct right, left, and center will inevitably get their dander up. Mission accomplished!

Overture

In Honor Of Larry Kramer For Writing *Faggots*

Truth And Dare
De Gustibus Non Est Disputandum

Legal Disclaimer, Before You Read Further:

Being a staunch conservative-libertarian, capitalist and anticommunist, with an unshakable faith in free market economies and the right of individual self-determination, I am a fervent devotee of and believer in the *free market of ideas*; however right or wrong my or your ideas may or may not be. As such, I am a strong enthusiast and practitioner of *fallibilism*; so, anything I postulate hereafter is fair game for personal or scholarly umbrage or critique—and, indeed, is even encouraged to be haughtily dismissed as the debauched, demented rantings and ravings of a mad man. **You should understand that this is simply me ruminating and that I don't necessarily believe any of the claptrap put forward henceforth; I have no ideology and no particular axe to grind *per se*, so you are free to read into this work whatever you like or dislike. It understood that I am the consummate Devil's Advocate and *Heresiarch*, this is theoretical experimentation, not necessarily a testament of my personal faith; or, in other words, although this is a *weltanschauung*, it is no necessarily my *weltanschauung*. DE PROFUNDIS: *to think* something is not the same as *to believe* something. Comprehende? Therefore, because I am not interested in *evincing* or convincing you, converting you, persuading you, dissuading you, influencing you, swaying you,** changing you, turning you, proselytizing to you, propagandizing to you, or even interested in having you see my conjectural point of view, you are free to end this reading at any time and free to "BURN THIS BOOK" at your own leisure. Again, I don't need your fucking stamp of approval! *STET*

Raison d'être

Heterosexual Supremacy: Cult Of Perpetuity
Why The World Is Currently A Dystopia, How It Got To Be That Way
And What, If Anything, Can Be Done About It

The world is a tragedy to those who feel, and a comedy to those who think.
—William Shakespeare

It being axiomatic that one man's Dystopia is another man's Utopia (vice-versa and versa-vice), *faute de meiux*, here is a purposely impious hypothesis.

In this avant-garde syllogistic treatise confronting the ineffable, I posit that the world is currently a Dystopia: 1.) *Heterosexual Supremacy* gives rise from whole cloth to the pseudoscience *Scientific Heterosexism*, 2.) the pseudoscience *Scientific Heterosexism* is used to manipulate the nexus-power-levers Politics, Law, Religion and Medicine to give legal cover for violent imposition of an authoritarian and totalitarian heterosexual Utopia, and 3.) this violently imposed totalitarian and authoritarian heterosexual Utopia self-perpetuates unawares, resulting in *The Heterosexual Manifesto*. Finally, in this avant-garde syllogistic treatise confronting the ineffable, I attempt to explain what, if anything, can be done about *The Heterosexual Manifesto*. With that, let me begin by defining the root cause of *The Heterosexual Manifesto*, which is, indeed, *Heterosexual Supremacy*.

Heterosexual Supremacy is a self-perpetuating, virulent, violent, totalitarian hate cult based solely on an extreme phobia and hate of male homosexuality. (Note,

I did not say it is based solely on an extreme phobia and hate of homosexuality, I said it is based solely on an extreme phobia and hate of *male* homosexuality; this distinction cannot be overstated and is critical to understanding the extreme complexity of *Heterosexual Supremacy*.) This self-perpetuating, virulent, violent, totalitarian hate cult based solely on an extreme phobia and hate of male homosexuality is a particularly dexterous, very infectious, supercilious agent that has secretly infected the body of human civilization. Stealthy, highly contagious and doctrinal; because *Heterosexual Supremacy* has surreptitiously acclimatized 99.9% of the human population, it is unquestioningly assumed to be the so-called norm when in reality it is the exception (especially in males), and is unquestioningly assumed to be the so-called cure when in reality it is the disease (especially in males). In fact, Heterosexual Supremacy is an incognito, elusive, malignant cancer, a sly, vague, cruel cancer that has metastasized throughout the entire body of human civilization—so much so that the hidden, subtle, malicious cancer, *Heterosexual Supremacy*, is mistaken for the body of human civilization, and the body of human civilization, *Knowledge*, is mistaken for the concealed, murky, wicked cancer.

That you cannot even momentarily suspend disbelief of the above juxtaposition is proof positive that manifest *Heterosexual Supremacy* is an indisputable *fait accompli*. But, not to worry, your heterosexual trance is natural. That's right, I said natural. (Well, perhaps you should worry, because I have come to the astonishing revelation that *natural doesn't necessarily mean good and unnatural doesn't necessarily mean bad; all, of course, depending on who's defining natural and unnatural, and good and bad*—and that, of course, all depends on who wins; and that, of course, primarily depends on who has the most money!) Heterosexual Supremacy, *compulsory heterosexuality*, is not an immaculate conception but an immaculate deception, and I am the first and only human being to date to expose it as such.

Anyway, the only thing you should understand is that humanity's state of Heterosexual Supremacy came about organically, spontaneously, haphazardly, subtly and, most importantly, without Machiavellian group machination or by some grand group conspiracy or design. Heterosexual Supremacy is an unplanned, amorphous, and totally self-sustaining cult that has insensibly codified through accidental inculcation and in turn petrified through involuntary indoctrination; it is not some ancient, on-going, never ending well planned out grand cabal. *Understand that humanity's descent into Heterosexual Supremacy was not Orwellian but Kafkaesque.* (Cancer, like life itself, isn't a grand conspiracy or necessarily organized; cancer is seemingly like entropy.

It just kind of sneaks up on you, overruns you, engulfs you and, before you know it, you're a goner.) In short, Heterosexual Supremacy is where we are today and where we are today is because wherever we are today is where we are supposed to be today. That's right, our current state of rampant, systematized Heterosexual Supremacy happened because it was *currently* meant to be—just like my eventual death and your eventual death, by God only knows what means, are *currently* meant to be.

Ah, now you're starting to see. Just because something is currently meant to be doesn't necessarily mean it is good. (Good for you, good for me, or good for humanity.) If you get cancer, it was currently meant to be, right? (You wouldn't have gotten it if it wasn't currently meant to be; that would be clearly illogical. And if you go into remission, that was currently meant to be; or should you die, that was currently meant to be etc.) So, you see, what is currently meant to be and what is not currently meant to be are opposite ends of a double edged sword:

Natural; *Currently* Meant To Be; *Currently* Exist
Unnatural; *Currently* Not Meant To Be; *Currently* Does Not Exist

And, as noted above, all of this plays out in the space-time continuum; what exist, what is natural, what is *currently* meant to be today, may not exist, may not be natural, may not be meant to be tomorrow. (I don't need to remind you that change is the only constant, do I? For example, catastrophic epidemics and pandemics of death by bubonic plague existed, were natural, were meant to be at one time in human history, but no longer exist, are not natural, are not currently meant to be today, because we now have antibiotics. *Quod Erat Demonstrandum.*) That understood, what I should have written above more explicitly is that Heterosexual Supremacy *currently* exist, Heterosexual Supremacy is *currently* natural, Heterosexual Supremacy is *currently* meant to be. In other words, because change is the only constant, *Heterosexual Supremacy is merely a temporary human happenstance and will inevitably evolve into something different.* Evolve into what exactly, I don't know. I only know this—change is *inexorable*; resistance to change is futile. Heterosexual Supremacy is no more immune from change than you or I are immune from death. But before I detail Heterosexual Supremacy's unavoidable evolution, let me take the opportunity to outline how we as human beings naturally arrived at the *current* sexually fascist state, Heterosexual Supremacy, that we live in and how we naturally obtained our *current* sexually phobic state of mind.

The Hand That Rocks The Hand That Rocks The Cradle

The trouble with thinkers—the innovators, the iconoclasts, the idea producers—is their detestable habit of asking "Why?" In their freewheeling style of fact finding, crap detecting, and idea producing, they continually overturn the applecarts of tradition and dogma. They threaten the comfortable predictability of custom by proposing things we have never tried before. They frighten us; they jar our sense of the "rightness" and stability of things. They can even question something as basic as motherhood. And most people don't like them for it.

—Karl Albrecht

Let's review. For extreme clarity's sake, what *succinctly* is Heterosexual Supremacy?

Heterosexual Supremacy is the all consuming, systemic and systematic, overt and subliminal psycho-sociological indoctrinated hatred of male homosexuality.

In short, as I said before, Heterosexual Supremacy is a totalitarian hate cult; albeit a self-staining one that has, unfortunately, overtly and subliminally inculcated and acclimatized most of the human population. When I wrote earlier that Heterosexual Supremacy is not some grand cabal, what I should have written with greater perspicuity is that Heterosexual Supremacy did not start out as a conspiracy—but, that it has, through conscious and unconscious (subliminal) indoctrination, regrettably, *devolved* into a conspiracy, a pernicious conspiracy but an *open conspiracy*—an *open conspiracy* of silence. How did this *open conspiracy* come about? Well, painful to say, it came about naturally. It is meant to be. Or, more precisely, it is *currently* meant to be; because, and it cannot be overstated, what is meant to be and what is not meant to be, i.e. what is natural and what is unnatural, are not set in stone but are in a constant state of flux. Regardless, the question remains, how *exactly* did we get to this *currently* natural totalitarian state of Heterosexual Supremacy that we are all in. The answer is Motherhood.

Current human biology, current human physiology and, most importantly, *current human sexual biomechanics* could only lead to the current state of Heterosexual Supremacy that we currently all suffer under. It's that simple. Unfortunately, the biological burden for gestating, incubating and birthing humans currently falls solely to females, and females currently have absolutely nothing to gain, biologically, from *male* homosexuality and currently have everything to lose, biologically, from *male* homosexuality—because of the current *physiological requirement and sexual biomechanics* that a male actually get and sustain an erection for intercourse and then orgasm inside of her vagina, the female is currently, physiologically, literally at the mercy of an ostensibly *heterosexual* male for procreative purposes; since a *homosexual* male cannot get an erection for intercourse, let alone sustain an erection for intercourse, and then orgasm inside of her. Conversely, males currently have absolutely nothing to lose, biologically, from *female* homosexuality and currently have everything to gain, biologically, from *female* homosexuality—because there currently is no *physiological or sexual biomechanical requirement* that a female do anything other than just lay there and be inseminated, the male is currently, physiologically, totally not at the mercy of a *heterosexual* female for procreative purposes; since a lesbian could just a well lay there an be inseminated as any straight woman could. Due to the current *physiological and sexual biomechanical differences* in the sexuality of males and females, the female is currently always at a distinct *physiological disadvantage* whenever there is male homosexuality and the male is inversely currently always at a distinct *physiological advantage* whenever there is female homosexuality. Therefore, the irrefutable fact that the female currently needs ostensibly *heterosexual male biomechanics* for intercourse to procreate, but the male does not need ostensibly heterosexual female biomechanics for intercourse to procreate—*because there is no such thing as heterosexual female biomechanics*—is thus the exact cause and effect, the means and end of our current totalitarian state of Heterosexual Supremacy = ***the all consuming, systemic and systematic, overt and subliminal psycho-sociological indoctrinated hatred of male homosexuality.***

Male = has a *sexual biomechanical requirement* for intercourse.
—Does not need a heterosexual female to conceive.

Female = does not have a *sexual biomechanical requirement* for intercourse.
—Needs a heterosexual male to conceive.

Homosexual Male = cannot meet *sexual biomechanical requirement* for *heterosexual* intercourse.
—Cannot conceive.

Lesbian = does not have a *sexual biomechanical requirement* for intercourse.
—Needs a heterosexual male to conceive.

But enough with all this *sexual biomechanics* logic mumbo-jumbo and intellectual high-mindedness. Let's get down to the real nitty-gritty. In the end, human evolution is only concerned with one thing:

Strength (Potency) = a stiff dick—Versus—Weakness (Impotency) = a limp dick

That's it in a nutshell (you'll excuse the rhetorical irony). In layman's terms, with strength (potency), the human race survives and prospers, without strength (impotency), the human race withers and becomes extinct—and, with that understood, only the homosexual male is (at least currently) in a biologically indefensible position. (**Because of the *sexual biomechanical requirement* that always and only applies to the male, if every male in the world were homosexual, the human race would go extinct; yet, because the female has no *sexual biomechanical requirement*, if every male in the world were heterosexual but every female in the world were lesbian, the human race would easily survive. *Quod Erat Demonstrandum*.**) Therefore, listen up all you bra burning so-called feminists: IN (CURRENT) HUMAN EVOLUTION, STRENGTH HAS ALL VALUE AND WEAKNESS HAS NO VALUE; THEREFORE, THE ERECT PENIS (OF THE OSTENSIBLY HETEROSEXUAL MALE) HAS GREATER VALUE THAN THE VAGINA—SINCE, FOR PROCREATIVE PURPOSES, IT DOESN'T MATTER IF THE VAGINA IS LESBIAN OR HETEROSEXUAL.

In other words, for current procreative purposes, because the *heterosexual* male is indispensable, the male is indispensable; but, for current procreative purposes, because the sexuality of the particular female is irrelevant, the female is notionally irrelevant. Pretty tough stuff to take, isn't it? Well, I don't make the *rules of sexual biomechanics*, I just write about them. Needless to say, the homosexual male is human evolution's wild card or joker and, as such, he is scapegoated at every turn. The only thing you should understand is that paramount to current human evolution is this concept of strength (potency) versus weakness (impotency). Because, currently, "weakness" has absolutely no value and, currently, "strength" has all value, "weakness" in any form is currently a direct threat to the survival of the human species. In example, because the homosexual male cannot get an erection for procreative purposes, he is currently a direct threat to the survival of the human species. (Did I just write those words?! Yes, I think I did.) Anyway, understanding strength (potency) versus weakness (impotency), you now clearly see why the over-arching mandates necessary to Motherhood—*the sexual biomechanical requirement that exist only for males that is necessary to achieve pregnancy for females*—is the generator of Heterosexual Supremacy, and why the homosexual male is solely detested and violently attacked, but the lesbian is generally treated with an indifferent shrug or meet with only cursory, perfunctory *feigned* protests.

Although both male and female are technically obligatory for human procreation, because the female has no *sexual biomechanical requirement* for intercourse, the female is always, without question, a minor, negligible, immaterial, replaceable and partially-dispensable character in the grand play that is human procreation; thus, *female* homosexuality is simply not seen as a threat to human survival and not seen gravely or really-truly taken seriously the way *male* homosexuality is. Essentially, *female* homosexuality will never have the same cache that *male* homosexuality has when it comes to sheer venomous fear and loathing, because the female has no *sexual biomechanical requirement* for intercourse but the male does—making the male an always major, indispensable, irreplaceable character in the grand play that is human procreation, but the female an always inconsequential, nondescript, replaceable, fairly-expendable character in the grand play that is human procreation. So, it is clear to see why humanity inherently has an obsessive-compulsive terror of only *male* homosexuality. As a matter of fact, the only reason *female* homosexuality is ever really attacked, if it is ever really attacked at all, is because such a thing as *male* homosexuality exist; in other words, if *male* homosexuality didn't exist, people would have no problem with *female* homosexuality; *id est*, the only reason people object to female homosexuality is because to not object to *female* homosexuality is essentially to give license to *male* homosexuality, and license to *male* homosexuality can never be given; *id est*, the only reason female homosexuality is not accepted is because acceptance of *female* homosexuality would mean acceptance of *male* homosexuality, and acceptance of *male* homosexuality is always a bridge too far. So, in summation, any fury and opposition people have towards *female* homosexuality is always wholly dependent on and always solely predicated on any fury and opposition people have towards *male* homosexuality. *Quod Erat Demonstrandum.*

Coming To Terms With Human Evolution's Odd-Man-Out

For you to read any further requires that you get a crash course in *Sexology*; which is essentially a comprehension that meticulously does not, in any way, shape or form, idealize, romanticize, and sentimentalize human sexuality. *Sexology* is an extremely rigorous medical and academic field that takes a purely scientific, clinical, empirical, warts-and-all, in-depth approach to human sexuality. (To be a *Sexologist*, you must have an M.D. or, at least, a Ph.D.) You can get a crash course in *Sexology* by reading *Gay, Straight And In-Between*, by the undeniably flawed but indisputably brilliant Sexologist Dr. John Money. The only drawback you should be aware of, however, is that *Gay, Straight And In-Between* is not written for the layman and is not written in layman's terms; but is inflexibly written for medical academics and stringently written using medical and academic argot. Nevertheless, it is my very strong belief, that *Gay, Straight And In-Between* is essential reading, should you wish to continue with this treatise.

Gay, Straight, And In-Between
By John Money, Ph.D. (John Hopkins University & Hospital)
Oxford University Press
ISBN: 0-19-505407-5

Hopefully, having read *Gay, Straight And In-Between*, now that you understand *Sexology*, you can begin to comprehend the parameters of Heterosexual Supremacy; primarily, what it is—***the all consuming, systemic and systematic, overt and subliminal psycho-sociological indoctrinated hatred of male homosexuality***—and, more importantly, how we got to this totalitarian state: we got to Heterosexual Supremacy *naturally*, because males currently have a *sexual biomechanical requirement*, thus making males completely indispensable, but females currently do not have a *sexual biomechanical requirement*, thus making females at least partially-dispensable. All this understood, we need to come to terms with the fact that the homosexual male, at least as he is currently construed, is in a biologically untenable position. (Note: the next sentence may seem like I am talking down to you, but I assure you, I am not.) **Because your *enculturation* inherently inhibits you from truly grasping, let alone accepting, the sheer mercilessness, the sheer cruelty, the sheer brutality, the sheer randomness, and the sheer mind-numbing complexity of life, understanding the evolutionary conundrum of the homosexual male, at least as he is currently construed, will be extremely difficult for you; therefore, from here onward I will be using** *literary dialectical algorithms* **to, hopefully, help you along:**

Sexual Realpolitik

**An Analytic & Computational Theorem Of *The Heterosexual Manifesto*
And What, If Anything, Can Be Done About It**

Dedicated To Aristotle For Being A Mathematician First And Foremost

---

The great masses of the people will more easily fall victims to a
great lie than to a small lie.

—Adolf Hitler

Axiom 1 LIFE IS INHERENTLY INEQUATABLE

A. THE UNIVERSE IS INTRINSICALLY ENTROPIC

— With an understanding that change is the only constant, the
Universe is in a never ending flux of going from a state of
disorder to a state of more disorder. The Universe never goes
from a state of disorder to a state of order, never goes from a state
of order to a state of disorder, and/or never goes from a state
of order to a state of more order. To overcome entropy (going
from a state of disorder to a state of more disorder) requires
rigor and rigor requires strength; therefore, in the Universe,
strength has all value and weakness had no value.

1. Entropy = Randomness
2. Randomness = Disorder
3. Disorder = Weakness

4. Weakness = To Not Adapt & Evolve

---

1. Problem Prevention & Problem Solving = Change
2. Change = Order
3. Order = Strength
4. Strength = To Adapt & Evolve

B. BECAUSE OF ENTROPY, THE INEQUITY OF LIFE IS PERMANENT

Denying that life is inherently inequitable only *exacerbates* the inherent inequitableness of life. Since all humans are victims of circumstance, and thus not omnipotent, humans cannot totally "end" the inherent inequitableness of life per se; humans can only *not* make the inherent inequitableness of life worse by *not* denying the inherent inequitableness of life. *Not* denying the inherent inequitableness of life does not mean simply throwing-up your hands in exasperation, disgust, resignation and defeat, or turning to nihilism or anarchy et al, nor does it mean becoming a cynic etc.; but, instead, accepting that life is inherently inequitable is the very foundation and the very basis to build upon the only constant, which is change = problem prevention and problem solving.

— Human beings do not have control over life; human beings only have control over their *response* to life.

1. By *not* denying that life is inherently inequitable, you make change for the better.
2. By denying that the life is inherently inequitable, you make change for the worse.
3. Whether "you" deny the inherent inequitableness of life or not, change is going to come, because change is the only constant.
4. Because the Universe is random, *life* is always going from disorder to more disorder or from order to disorder (from weakness to more weakness or from strength to weakness); only by exception, i.e. sheer random good luck, does something, anything, in the Universe go from order to more order or from disorder to order (from strength to more strength or from weakness to strength).

1. *Life* is the exact opposite of a Meritocracy.
   - Because life is innately random, life is innately 51% luck and 49% pluck—note that luck always holds the controlling share; thus, "survival of the fittest" paradoxically means "survival of the luckiest."

2. *Life* is winner takes all.
   - Whoever wins gets to define the meaning of both words and actions; and thus gets to "enslave" the loser through the definition of words and actions.

     > Example: Whoever wins gets to define the meaning of "good" and "evil," since these are inherently existential and relative concepts; hence the always apropos phrase "Might makes right." (If Hitler had won WWII: 1.) you would be speaking German, and 2.) you would not be reading this book, because 3.) I would have never been born to write it; since 4.) my parents would have been exterminated before conceiving me. *Quod Erat Demonstrandum.*)

3. *The world* is inherently a Plutocracy
   - Knowledge = Money = Power
     Change is the only constant and money changes everything.

4. Natural Does Not Necessarily Mean Good
   - Natural; *Currently* Exist; *Currently* Meant To Be
     Natural = Logic = Change = Paradox = Providence

   Unnatural Does Not Necessarily Mean Bad
   - Unnatural; *Currently* Does Not Exist; *Currently* Not Meant To Be
     Unnatural = Illogic = Static = Contradiction = Entropy

   Example:

   It may be "logical," but is it good?

It may be "illogical," but is it bad?

Because Natural and Unnatural &
Good and Bad Are Inherently Relative And Existential:
    Natural and Unnatural & Good and Bad
    Are Solely Dependent On Who Is Defining
    Natural and Unnatural & Good and Bad

5. The nexus-power-levers Politics, Law, Religion, & Medicine are used (by
    whoever wins in the Plutocracy) to define words and actions, giving legal
    cover for VIOLENCE, to literally and physically make the world in the
    exact spitting image of the winner; in our case, the pseudoscience *Scientific
    Heterosexism* is used as the means to manipulate the nexus-power-levers
    Politics, Law, Religion & Medicine to define words and actions, giving
    legal cover for VIOLENCE, to literally and physically make the world in
    the exact spitting image of the heterosexual; resulting in a self-perpetuating
    heterosexual utopia, *The Heterosexual Manifesto*.

6. Monopolies are antithetical to the nature of the Universe and all of Life;
    Competition (which results in diversity, not the other way around) is
    the foundation of the Universe and all of Life.

    a. Sexual Monopolies are thus antithetical to the Universe and all of
        Life; compulsory heterosexuality is a sexual monopoly.

Axiom 2

From a current human evolutionary standpoint:

Strength (Order) Has All Value

    1. *Strength always must be earned; Strength is never a given!*
    2. *Strength is always in demand; demand always exceeds supply!*

Weakness (Disorder) Has No Value

    1. *Weakness is always a given; Weakness never needs to be earned!*
    2. *Weakness is never in demand; supply is always limitless!*

Axiom 3

From a current human evolutionary standpoint:

Strength = Potency = Masculine (Masculinity) = Male (Body & Behavior)
Weakness = Impotency = Feminine (Femininity) = Female (Body & Behavior)

Male/Masculine Sexual Psychology (Dominant/Aggressive):
Wants And Needs To Dominate **(In And Out Of The Bedroom)**

1. Because life is inherently inequitable, the masculine psyche inherently always operates from a position of strength—the masculine psyche *does not require* someone submissive (someone who wants and needs to be dominated); since the masculine psyche can just as well dominate someone dominant (someone who wants and needs to dominate). In other words, it is logically possible for a dominant to dominate a dominant, not just dominate a submissive. *Quod Erat Demonstrandum.*

Female/Feminine Sexual Psychology (Submissive/Passive):
Wants And Needs To Be Dominated **(In And Out Of The Bedroom)**

2. Because life is inherently inequitable, the feminine psyche inherently always operates from a position of weakness—the feminine psyche *requires* someone dominant (someone who wants and needs to dominate); since it is not logically possible to be dominated by someone submissive (someone who wants and needs to be dominated). In other words, it is not logically possible for a submissive to dominate a submissive (let alone for a submissive to dominate a dominant). *Quod Erat Demonstrandum.*

Lastly, There Is No Incongruity In Masculine/Feminine Sexual Psychology:

1. If you *want and need to dominate* in the bedroom; you *want and need to dominate* out of the bedroom.
2. If you *want and need to be dominated* in the bedroom; you *want and need to be dominated* out of the bedroom.

Axiom 4

From a current human evolutionary standpoint, because weakness has no value, the female inherently has no value—except for the sole purpose of human procreation:

1. The "Female Body" only has value for the sole purpose of human procreation.
2. "Female Behavior" (Femininity; Weakness) has no value, and is only "tolerated" in the sole context of the "Female Body."
3. "Female Behavior" (Femininity; Weakness) is "tolerated" in the sole context of the "Female Body" only because the "Female Body" is absolutely necessary for procreative purposes.

    Exhibit A: If "Female Behavior" (Femininity; Weakness) had any value outside the sole context of the "Female Body," the Effeminate Male would be exulted and worshipped, but instead the Effeminate Male is near universally violently loathed, violently derided and violently despised. *Quod Erat Demonstrandum.*

    Exhibit B: The Masculine Female is either met with a collective shrug or a hearty pat on the back for being ballsy enough to "trade up"—unlike the Effeminate Male, who is angrily considered craven for supposedly having "traded down." *Quod Erat Demonstrandum.*

4. Were the "Female Body" not absolutely necessary for procreative purposes, "Female Behavior" (Femininity; Weakness) would not be "tolerated" in the female; indeed, were the "Female Body" not absolutely necessary for procreative purposes, the "Female Body" itself would be considered superfluous. Thus, from a current human evolutionary standpoint, "weakness," in the form of the "Female Body," is "femininity's" only "strength" and it's only reason for being in existence.

Axiom 5

From a current human evolutionary standpoint, the homosexual male inherently has no value, since he does not and cannot procreate:

1. The inherently valueless effeminate homosexual male fundamentally has even less value than the inherently valueless masculine homosexual male; because "Female Behavior" (Femininity; Weakness) inherently has no value, and is only "tolerated" in the context of the "Female Body" and is only "tolerated" because the "Female Body" is absolutely necessary for procreative purposes. Concerning human procreation, the *sexual biomechanical requirement* currently always and only applies to the male, and male homosexual orientation does not allow for fulfilling this requirement.

   Addendum: Since, from a current human evolutionary standpoint, "weakness" (Female Behavior; Femininity) is inherently valueless, and only "tolerated" in the context of the "Female Body" and only because the "Female Body" is absolutely necessary for human procreation, the effeminate homosexual male, contrary to politically correct mythology, is never transgressive but wholly and always counterproductive. (Now, the *Transgender Thought Police* will inevitably come after me and say this statement is so-called "hate speech" and that I am a "self-loathing" homosexual male (that I have so-called *internalized homophobia*) etc. and demand I be excommunicated from the Gay Tribe. Well, if being a Heresiarch and "thinking whatever the hell I want to think" is a crime, then I plead guilty. The *Transgender Thought Police* really need to get over themselves and their outrageous refusal to deal with the harsh physical realities of life, logic and illogic, by descending into the psychosis of *physical relativism. Behavior* is physical and it therefore cannot be *relative*; that would be like saying that violent behavior is the exact same as non-violent behavior, which is clearly illogical.) The effeminate male, the transgender male, the transsexual, the transvestite, whatever you want to call him (or her); none of them have any value in the evolutionary scheme of things; and all of them are inherently counterproductive. As I said before, I don't make the *rules of sexual biomechanics,* I just write about them.

2. The inherently valueless masculine homosexual male fundamentally has greater value than the even more inherently valueless effeminate homosexual male; because "Masculine Behavior" (Masculinity; Strength) inherently has all value, but "Female Behavior" (Femininity; Weakness) inherently has no value, and is only "tolerated" in the context of the "Female Body" and is only "tolerated" because the

"Female Body" is absolutely necessary for procreative purposes. Concerning human procreation, although he may be masculine, the *sexual biomechanical requirement* currently always and only applies to the male, and male homosexual orientation does not allow for fulfilling this requirement.

3. The Lesbian (whether masculine or feminine) can procreate all she wants, since, as a female, she has no *sexual biomechanical requirement*; thus, from a current human evolutionary standpoint, the Lesbian always has value, while the homosexual male (regardless whether he is masculine or feminine) never has value, since the homosexual male cannot fulfill the *sexual biomechanical requirement* of males. *Quod Erat Demonstrandum.*

Axiom 6

From a current human evolutionary standpoint, the definition of Masculinity (Strength) and Femininity (Weakness) and the worth of Strength versus Weakness, however unfair, is based in logic, not biology:

1. Some so-called feminists have tried to *redefine* what femininity means (inside and outside the context of the "Female Body") and have tried to give femininity all kinds of positive connotations; but logic dictates that "femininity" is synonymous with "weakness" (and "weakness" has no value).

2. Some so-called feminists refuse to equate femininity with weakness and instead equate femininity with strength—circular logic that ironically disproves their feminist argument, since they obviously feel that "strength" is a good thing and "weakness" is a bad thing.

3. Some so-called feminists have tried to *redefine* what masculinity means (inside and outside the context of the "Male Body") and have tried to give masculinity all kinds of negative connotations; but logic dictates that "masculinity" is synonymous with "strength" (and "strength" has all value).

4. Some so-called feminists refuse to equate masculinity with strength and instead equate masculinity with weakness—circular logic that ironically disproves their feminist argument, since they obviously feel that "weakness" is a bad thing and "strength" is a good thing.

Axiom 7

From a current human evolutionary standpoint, "weakness" (Female Behavior; Femininity)—which is only "tolerated" in the context of the "Female Body" and only "tolerated" because the "Female Body" is absolutely necessary for procreative purposes—is humanity's and human evolution's *bete noire*:

1. From a current human evolutionary standpoint, because the homosexual male (whether masculine or feminine) cannot have sex with the female (by being priapic), he will always and forever be associated with "weakness" (impotency); and, remember, "weakness" (Female Behavior; Femininity) is only "tolerated" in the context of the "Female Body" and it is only "tolerated" because the "Female Body" is absolutely necessary for procreative purposes.

2. From a current human evolutionary standpoint, because "weakness" (Female Behavior; Femininity) has no value, and is only "tolerated" in the context of the Female Body and is only "tolerated" because the "Female Body" is absolutely necessary for procreative purposes, the effeminate homosexual male must understand that he especially has absolutely no value and thus must take swift and radical proactive steps to *self-actualize* to deal with the severe situation he has been thrown in.

3. From a current human evolutionary standpoint, the masculine homosexual male must come to terms with understanding that no matter how masculine he is, he has no value and cannot be considered the equal of a heterosexual male; and the masculine homosexual male must learn to deal with the slings and arrows, both physical and verbal, that are almost always only directed toward the effeminate homosexual male, but inadvertently strike him.

Axiom 8

What is natural today may not be natural tomorrow; the Space-Time Continuum is omnipotent and omnipresent:

1. From a current human evolutionary standpoint, the "Female Body" (regardless of sexual orientation) is *currently* absolutely necessary for procreative purposes, but the "Female Body" may not be absolutely

    necessary for procreative purposes tomorrow; and that would be "natural."

2. From a current human evolutionary standpoint, the ostensibly Heterosexual Male is *currently* rationally necessary for procreative purposes, but the ostensibly Heterosexual Male may not be rationally necessary for procreative purposes tomorrow; and that would be "natural."

3. From a current human evolutionary standpoint, the Homosexual Male *currently* cannot procreate, but that may not be the case tomorrow; and that would be "natural."

4. Axiom 8 can, at any time, take precedence over all other axioms; because "change is the only constant," what may be true (natural; logical) today, may not be true (natural; logical) tomorrow, ironically, including this very statement. Time (change) stands still for no one; so, you can either get out of its way or be flattened by it—resistance is futile.

5. Since "change is the only constant," the word "CURRENT" is always *understood* (as in, it is always a given) and does not always need to be actually, literally stated and is usually only actually, literally stated for emphasis purposes—so, henceforth, in this work, the word *current* will only be used for accent functions.

6. Because change is *inexorable,* the only question is will be there be change for the better or will there be change for the worse—and that, of course, is wholly dependent on who is defining "better" and who is defining "worse." ***Quod Erat Demonstrandum.***

We are discreet sheep; we wait to see how the drove is going, and then we go with the drove. We have two opinions: one private, which we are afraid to express; and another one—the one we use—which we force ourselves to wear to please Mrs. Grundy, until habit makes us comfortable in it, and the custom of defending it presently makes us love it, adore it, and forget how pitifully we came by it.

—Mark Twian

Stop! Take a breather. The next axiom and following axioms are truly perilous ones for the reader. Because "mother" and "motherhood" are *currently* considered sacred and sanctified in human civilization, the next axiom and following axioms should be approached very gingerly—if approached at all. Because we all have been born/borne by a mother, because we all have been born/borne to a mother, and because we, most likely, all have been raised with and by a mother, it is understandable that we hold "mother" and "motherhood" in such reflexive high esteem. Nevertheless, because no one and no group is beyond reproach, an arithmetical analysis of "mother" and "motherhood" is essential to detailing the syllogism that is The Heterosexual Manifesto. Thus, "mother" and "motherhood" cannot be spared questioning; so, you should seriously pause and reflect before considering the next axioms. (Again, let me say that I am not talking down to you. Out of an abundance of caution, I like to give people a heads-up before I send them reeling.) Because of your *enculturation*—self-serving, but intrinsically self-defeating, subliminal indoctrination by human civilization—you will almost certainly take extreme offense at and not be able to grasp the meaning of the upcoming axioms, especially if you haven't done some mental and emotional preparatory work first. So, I strongly urge to you prep, prep, prep! **To appreciate the acuity of the upcoming axioms, and not be hospitalized for hyperventilating, you must first throw off the shackles of your *enculturation* and become neurosis-free; and the quickest way to help accomplish this startling feat of mental and emotional acrobatics is to apply the principles in the magnum opus *The Sky's The Limit*, by none other than the indispensable Dr. Wayne W. Dyer.** Nuff said. If you have not mentally and emotionally prepped or refuse to mentally and emotionally prep, proceed to the upcoming axioms at your own risk.

Axiom 9

From a current human evolutionary standpoint, because the female, regardless of sexual orientation, has everything to lose and nothing to gain by male homosexuality, and because the female solely gestates, incubates and gives births to children, the female *overtly and subliminally inculcates* an extreme hatred of *male* homosexuality, and only *male* homosexuality, to the child, whether she knows it or not, simply by her mere biological presence; ergo, motherhood and the female archetype, at least as they are currently construed and have been for millennia, are the very genesis of Heterosexual Supremacy that inevitably results in *The Heterosexual Manifesto*. Most importantly, through her mere biological presence, the female, both overtly and subliminally, instills a *paranoid sense of obligation* in the male child to be sexually attracted to females (and only females)—i.e. "If I am not sexually attracted to females (and only females), it must mean that I hate my mother, the person who carried

and nurtured me in her womb for x amount of months and then went through excruciating pain to deliver me into this world."

Aide memoire: Axioms 2 & 3—Femininity (female body and behavior) is weakness; weakness has no value; thus, the female has no value; therefore, femininity is only "tolerated" in the sole context of the female body, and only "tolerated" because the female body is absolutely necessary for procreative purposes.

1.   The female, regardless of sexual orientation, subconsciously understands the dire implications of her birth as a female; namely, that femininity (female body and behavior) is weakness and that weakness inherently has no value, and that her only value is as a vassal for procreative purposes.

2.   Because femininity (female body and behavior) has no value, except for the sole context of human procreation, the female, regardless of sexual orientation, inherently always operates from a position of weakness (valueless-ness), and the female subconsciously understands this.

   A.   Subconsciously understanding the predicament of her birth, the heterosexual female makes a *Faustian* bargain to subjugate herself to the exclusively heterosexual male's domination, so long as he *violently* enforces Heterosexual Supremacy, perpetuating The Heterosexual Manifesto.

      1.   Because the heterosexual female understands explicitly that her only *saving grace*, as a female, is her sole ability to produce children (i.e. the only reason humanity keeps her, a female, around); 99.9% of heterosexual females are sociopaths who have made a conscious decision to subjugate themselves to the exclusively heterosexual male, so long as he does everything in his power to violently destroy male homosexuality (and only male homosexuality).

   B.   The lesbian, considered nothing more or less than a eunuch by her heterosexual female peers, is almost always dismissed, marginalized, patronized or just ignored with a truly indifferent shrug. Because the female has no sexual biomechanical requirement, the lesbian is considered a non-entity and the issue of lesbianism *per se* is considered a non-issue. In essence, as a threat to the survival of humanity, the lesbian is not taken seriously by heterosexual females and is secretly seen as a laughingstock for being neither fish nor foul and as harmless and benign as both.

3. Because monopolies are antithetical to the Universe and all of Life, the sexual monopoly that the female has on child birth must inexorably come to an end! Upon the inevitable invention of the *alternative human womb*, the female, regardless of sexual orientation, will become wholly superfluous—and this is her greatest fear; since the female, regardless of sexual orientation, subconsciously understands that the only value the female (feminine body and feminine behavior) has is as a vassal for human procreation.

    1. The Universe is inherently Entropic:
      — The Universe is in a constant flux of going from a state of disorder to a state of more disorder. The Universe never goes from a state of disorder to a state of order, never goes from a state of order to a state of disorder, and/or never goes from a state of order to a state of more order. (See Axiom 1.)

        1. Entropy = Randomness
        2. Randomness = Disorder
        3. Disorder = Weakness
        4. Weakness = Static

---

        1. Problem Prevention & Problem Solving = Change
        2. Change = Order
        3. Order = Strength
        4. Strength = Evolving

    2. To overcome the Entropy of the Universe requires rigor.
    3. Rigor always requires strength.

4. Female body and Female behavior are axiomatically the opposite of strength: weakness.

5. Therefore, because (in the Universe) strength has all value and weakness had no value, female body and female behavior will be superfluous once the female no longer has an inescapable monopoly on gestating, incubating, and birthing children—since the inescapable monopoly to gestate, incubate, and birth children is the only so-called "strength" that female body and female behavior have; and, indeed, as I said before, this inescapable monopoly to gestate, incubate, and birth children is the only reason that female body and female behavior are "tolerated" at all. Essentially, through this inescapable monopoly to gestate, incubate, and birth children, female body and female behavior have been holding all of humanity hostage and have been blackmailing all of humanity since time immemorial. The invention of the alternative human womb takes away the "trump card" of female body and female behavior, and essentially renders female body and female behavior obsolete and useless.

4. Eventual and inexorable removal of the female, regardless of sexual orientation, from the human procreative equation ends the genesis and maintenance of *Heterosexual Supremacy* that results in *The Heterosexual Manifesto*. (Reference Axioms 1 & 8 for greater clarity.)

5. The heterosexual female is axiomatically paranoid about male homosexuality, since the homosexual male offers an indisputable, inescapable, no-strings-attached sexual alternative to her own notional, always-strings-attached sexuality; however, because of the politically correct times in which we live, most present-day heterosexual females are very closeted about their *paranoia of male homosexuality*, and usually *feign* indifference or ambivalence about male homosexuality—with some even going so far as to *feign* fellowship and camaraderie with the homosexual male.

   A. The heterosexual female especially fears the *masculine* homosexual male, since he is immune to being a wretched object of scorn and ridicule; and is therefore a force to be reckoned with, and a direct threat to her sexual monopoly.

B. The heterosexual female does not envy or empathizes with the *effeminate* homosexual male, because she instinctively knows that femininity outside the sole context of the female body is always a non-starter, always seen as the opposite of sexually attractive (to all and sundry), and always seen as just plain pathetic. She understands that the effeminate homosexual male is an object of scorn and contempt (by all and sundry) because he is a mirror image of her without the ability to provide children, and therefore he is completely worthless, useless and is always treated as such. Frequently, the heterosexual female secretly delights in *schadenfreude* at the effeminate homosexual male's life of quiet desperation, as she thinks to herself, "There but for the grace of God (giving me breasts and female plumbing) go I."

C. The heterosexual female's *inherent paranoia of male homosexuality* can be either covert or overt, depending on here societal background and upbringing. If it is covert, it manifest itself in a toxic false indifference and ambivalence, while silently "policing" all boys for any effeminacy, and then subtly and silently using the exclusively heterosexual male as a proxy to enforce gender conformity, by way of violence, in any straying males. At the opposite end of the spectrum, someone like Ann Coulter, who exemplifies the heterosexual female's paranoia of *male* homosexuality, dispenses with the pretense of indifference altogether, and literally goes straight for the homosexual male's jugular (if not his testicles).

D. Because the female gestates incubates and births the human, she invariably uses this fact as a guilt-inducing-cudgel to silence her critics before they even dare begin. All males, but especially the exclusively heterosexual male, feel extraordinarily beholden to the female for her "labor" and consider it sacrilegious and blasphemous to even contemplate the possibility that the female as part of the birthing process may in fact now be a hindrance to continual human evolution. The heterosexual female is particularly adept at using the fact that she gives birth to children to instill this sense that somehow she is to be revered and worshipped, and that by extension all females are to be revered and worshipped for their supposed service to humanity. A homosexual male son is seen as an affront to her as female and a homosexual male son is seen as something of an ingrate; and all homosexual males are considered "freeloaders," since they aren't giving anything in return, namely a stiff cock, to other females.

Axiom 10

It clearly understood that Heterosexual Supremacy is a self-sustaining, psycho-sociological, totalitarian hate cult, the exclusively heterosexual male is not exclusively heterosexual innately or biologically but is in actuality only exclusively heterosexual by *systemic and systematic, overt and subliminal psycho-sociological indoctrinated design.* The exclusively heterosexual male is in fact exclusively heterosexual only superficially, because he is in reality inherently bisexual; however, his *heterosexual supremacist indoctrination* does not allow for him to know that he is inherently bisexual and, of course, his *heterosexual supremacist indoctrination* does not allow for him to know that he has, indeed, been indoctrinated. Because the supposedly heterosexual male has been indoctrinated into a *heterosexist state of being,* and did not come to his supposed exclusive heterosexuality innately, biologically, by sheer osmosis or by free will, he can be inadvertently advertently or advertently inadvertently *deprogrammed* serendipitously—and is hence strictly quarantined, both physically and psychologically, literally for his entire life (by the overt and subliminal *heterosexual supremacist superstructure*) from ever partaking in any actual homosexual sexual-activity, thus resulting in *latent* homosexuality. In other words, the exclusively heterosexual male is only exclusively heterosexual by default of being quarantined from ever even once partaking in any homosexual sexual-activity; and, should this quarantine be breached, all bets are off on his sexual orientation. Because the exclusively heterosexual male experiences latent homosexuality and cannot deal with it, due to his vicious heterosexist programming, 99.9% of exclusively heterosexual males are violent psychopaths who either manage to hide it well or who don't even bother with the pretense of civil affectation.

In summation:

1. Because of male physiology, all males are inherently bisexual.
2. The homosexual potential of the exclusively heterosexual male is unrealized.
3. Because the homosexual potential of the exclusively heterosexual male is unrealized, this results in severely repressed or latent homosexuality in the exclusively heterosexual male.
4. This severely repressed or latent homosexuality in the exclusively heterosexual male is represented by an extreme and obsessive hatred of effeminate males. (If the exclusively heterosexual male were truly inherently heterosexual, he would be sexually attracted to femininity, i.e. feminine behavior, in whatever its physical form.) The exclusively heterosexual male feels inner tumult over the fact that he is not attracted to both female form and function (not just the female body, but female behavior). Unable to reconcile the attraction-repulsion and repulsion-attraction of his own homosexual lust, the exclusively heterosexual male proceeds to *project* VIOLENCE in order to exercise his latent homosexual demons.
5. The extreme and obsessive hatred of effeminate males is sole—the exclusively heterosexual male is either indifferent or feels camaraderie with a masculine female or a lesbian; and rarely, if ever, feels threatened by a masculine female or a lesbian. The exclusively heterosexual male can not understand why he feels infinity or kinship for the masculine female or lesbian but feels nothing but repulsion, not sexual attraction nor kinship, for the effeminate male, and this sexual incongruence causes more inner sexual angst.
6. The exclusively heterosexual male's extreme and obsessive hatred of effeminate males leads him to violence of all homosexual males—all the while he is subconsciously lusting after the *masculine* male. (He may consciously be sexually attracted to the *female body*, because that is permissible by societal standards, but his attraction to both *masculine form and masculine behavior* remains buried deep in his subconscious, because that sexual attraction is strictly forbidden by societal standards. The exclusively heterosexual male's subconscious sexual attraction to *masculine form and masculine behavior* is manifest in a *Freudian Slip*: if he were forced to have sex with a male, he would prefer to have sex with a masculine male rather than with a feminine male (see in-depth example below). Violence against all homosexual

males becomes the means by which the exclusively heterosexual male outwardly expresses his repulsion at male effeminacy due to his severely repressed sexual lust for *masculine form and masculine behavior.*

1. The root cause of the exclusive heterosexual male's latent homosexuality is due to the inherent illogic of his systemic and systematic, overt and subliminal psycho-sociological indoctrinated *heterosexist sexual programming.*

    A. He cannot logically *reconcile* the fact he may be sexually attracted to the female body but is not sexually attracted solely to feminine behavior, and especially not sexually attracted to feminine behavior outside the sole context of the female body—as exemplified by his extreme repulsion at male effeminacy.

    B. He cannot psychologically *accept* the fact he is sexually attracted to masculine behavior and demeanor, and he cannot accept the fact that he is, at the very least, sexually intrigued by the *perfect male physique.*

        Example again: Most exclusively heterosexual males are in a constant state of subconscious turmoil over this fact and usually give themselves away with a *Freudian slip*: When you ask exclusively heterosexual males, if they were forced to have sex with a male, would they choose an effeminate male or a masculine male, they always choose the masculine male, and invariably say, "Having sex with an effeminate man is like having sex with a girl and if I wanted to have sex with a girl I would just have sex with a girl."

    C. All male *contact sports* and so-called "male bonding" are state sanctioned forms of homoeroticism that allow the exclusively heterosexual male to maintain the veneer of exclusive heterosexuality while expressing his latent homosexuality from a safe distance.

2. Having been, literally from birth, systemically and systematically, overtly and subliminally psycho-sociologically indoctrinated into exclusive heterosexuality, latent homosexuality in the exclusively heterosexual male manifest into *paranoia of male homosexuality*, and only male homosexuality. (Homophobia

is too quaint a term and doesn't properly convey the viciously indoctrinated psycho-pathology of the exclusively heterosexual male.) This *paranoia of male homosexuality*, and only male homosexuality, inevitably leads to extreme violence against those who are subconsciously perceived as a threat to his heterosexual supremacist programming.

3. Because of his vicious systemic and systematic, overt and subliminal psycho-sociological indoctrination, the exclusively heterosexual male only understands one language, the language VIOLENCE! The exclusively heterosexual male does not understand logic or reason, and civility and progress, because logic, reason, civility and progress dictate that change is the only constant (see Axiom 1); and thus logic, reason, civility and progress are always in direct conflict with his indoctrinated heterosexual supremacist programming.

4. The exclusively heterosexual male invented the *concept of religion* to help *violently impose* Heterosexual Supremacy, which perpetuates The Heterosexual Manifesto. Meaning that religion exist so long as only he, the exclusively heterosexual male, gets to define what is and what isn't religion. (Note the indisputable fact that all the Gods, Messiahs, Prophets, Saints, Martyrs etc. in all the major so-called Abrahamic religions are in his own violent, war-mongering, heterosexist image. *Quod Erat Demonstrandum.*) To buttress his *self-made concept of religion*, the exclusively heterosexual male insist there is such a thing as so-called *natural law* and then audaciously goes about solely defining this so-called *natural law* so that it mirrors his own heterosexual sexual aesthetics.

5. Because his exclusively heterosexual male psyche is an extremely fragile human psycho-sociological construct, not a reality, latent homosexuality causes a schism in the exclusively heterosexual male's persona, and it is for this reason that 99.9% of exclusively heterosexual males are psychopaths; albeit psychopaths running the asylum. His clear psychopathic symptoms of extreme narcissism, extreme remorselessness, extreme sense of entitlement, and extreme grandiosity (all exemplified by his making Gods in his own heterosexist image) come to the forefront when his latent homosexuality rears its pretty head, as he attempts to silence his inner homoerotic demons by

speaking in the only language that he knows and understands, VIOLENCE.

6. The exclusively heterosexual male uses the exclusively heterosexual female as something of a life raft and security blanket to shield him from his own homoerotic urges; the heterosexual female doesn't really exist for any purpose other than to validate and testify to the rest of world that he *is not*—as in, he *is not* a homosexual male, he is not a fag, he is not a supposed coward (i.e. he can "get it up" at the sight, taste and smell of female breasts and genitalia) etc.

Axiom 11

As long as Heterosexual Supremacy exist, inherently perpetuating The Heterosexual Manifesto, the homosexual male, and only the homosexual male, can never be properly and *peacefully* accepted or integrated into the current totalitarian heterosexual supremacist police state; therefore, the homosexual male must take radical actions to wholly separate from currently configured human civilization (The Heterosexual Manifesto).

In currently configured human civilization, male homosexuality is not solely about *being* (such as *being* Jewish or *being* Black), male homosexuality is most of all about *what homosexual males do*—and, more importantly, *what homosexual males don't do*; namely, get and maintain an erection at the supposedly titillating sight of breasts and female genitalia; thereby being able to procreate and propagate the human species. Because the female does not have a *sexual biomechanical requirement*, all of civilization is not built around her need for strength (an erect penis), which is why the lesbian is essentially a biological irrelevancy; where's all of civilization is built around the *sexual biomechanical requirement* that a male get and maintain an erection at the aforementioned breasts and female genitalia. (Again, if the entire population of males on planet earth were homosexual, then that theoretically would put the survival of the human species in peril, where's if the entire population of females on planet earth where lesbian, it doesn't theoretically reduce the chance of human survival at all, because the female has no *sexual biomechanical requirement* other than to lay down and be inseminated.) *The homosexual male is in a sui generis predicament primarily because he is male, not solely because he is homosexual.* Because only the male has a *sexual biomechanical requirement*, the homosexual male highlights the *sui generis* differentiation to that of a lesbian; thereby establishing that the homosexual male, and only the homosexual male, has irreconcilable differences with all of currently configured civilization (The Heterosexual Manifesto)—and society merely tinkering at the edges with human laws to decriminalize all homosexuality and legalize so-called gay marriage will not deny the fact that the homosexual male is in said *sui generis* predicament. For the homosexual male, and only the homosexual male, to be properly accepted into currently configured human civilization, currently configured human civilization would have to cease to exist and would, indeed, have to be turned upside down, downside up, inside out and outside in—and by this I mean the female, who is considered virtually sacrosanct in currently configured civilization, would have to be permanently and totally removed from the human gestating, incubating and child-birthing process altogether. Billions upon billions of people (who have been indoctrinated and brainwashed from conception into so-called religion) would have to be reoriented overnight into a whole new understanding of what it actually means to be a moral and upright human being; what it means to be a so-called man and what it means to be a so-called woman; what it means to be a so-called mother, what it means to be a so-called father, what it means to be a so-called child; essentially what it means to be a human being. Until and unless this complete and utter radical overturning of currently configured civilization—reorienting billions upon billions of people—actually ever happens, the homosexual male, and only the homosexual male, really only has but one choice: autonomy.

Remember, it's not about *being* a homosexual male, it's about what homosexual males *do* and, most importantly, what homosexual males *don't* *do* that can not be reconciled with currently configured civilization (The Heterosexual Manifesto):

1. Because of the *sexual biomechanical requirement* that exist only for males, male and female heterosexuality are irreconcilable with male homosexuality; lesbianism, a biological irrelevancy, is always reconcilable with male and female heterosexuality, and, indeed, is part of the subconscious veneer of exclusive male heterosexuality. (Example: Note that lesbian porn is always categorized by academicians as only inside the *canon* of heterosexual porn, never categorized inside the *canon* of homosexual porn.)

2. Because male and female heterosexuality are irreconcilable with male homosexuality (and only male homosexuality), Heterosexual Supremacy is inevitable, resulting in The Heterosexual Manifesto.

3. The homosexual male must be "lucky" enough to fully grasp the *sui generis* implications of his birth as a homosexual male, and be both "lucky" and "plucky" enough to take the radical actions, though

agonizing and arduous, necessary to wholly separate himself from currently configured civilization (The Heterosexual Manifesto).

A. The exclusively heterosexual male, and his sycophant, the heterosexual female, cannot be reasoned with (See Axiom 11); and the exclusively heterosexual male's unwitting accomplice, the lesbian, is clueless of her own unfortunate stake in Heterosexual Supremacy.

4. Ultimately, the homosexual male is his own worst enemy and all his wounds are self-inflicted—by his refusal to acknowledge the *sui generis* nature of his birth as a homosexual male and take the appropriate actions to mitigate this fact. Instead of thinking and acting logically to prevent and solve his *sui generis* problems, however agonizing that may be, the homosexual male instead descends into an extreme state of denial, extreme escapist thinking, extreme nihilism, extreme *solipsism*, extreme self-delusion, extreme self-loathing, extreme masochism, and extreme cowardice. At the top of the list of the homosexual male's craven and self-defeating actions is his refusal to acknowledge that, especially when-push-comes-to-shove, the exclusively heterosexual male speaks and understands only one language, the langue VIOLENCE.

5. The homosexual male must understand and accept the fact that femininity (feminine behavior) is exclusively reserved for the sole context of the female body, and whenever there is femininity outside the sole context of the female body, it is never seen as nurturing nor as sexually attractive or erotic; but that feminine behavior outside the sole context of the female body is always, always seen as a combination of spinelessness, gutlessness, pusillanimousness, timorousness *and* as trifling, frivolous, trivial, inconsequential, silly, superficial, sexually repulsive, and wholly 100% useless—and therefore seen as a direct threat to the survival of the human species! (See axiom 4 for greater clarity.)

6. The homosexual male must understand and accept that, because of the *sexual biomechanical requirement* of only males, lesbianism is not merely the opposite of male homosexuality but that *lesbianism is neutered male heterosexuality*; and therefore part of Heterosexual Supremacy that inevitably curdles into The Heterosexual Manifesto. (A lesbian woman is always considered to have *traded up* but a homosexual man is always considered to have *traded down*; thus,

male homosexuality will never receive the same *laisez faire* attitude accorded that of lesbianism. This is a painful but indisputable fact that the homosexual male simply has to deal with.)

7. Because femininity (feminine behavior) is exclusively reserved for the sole context of the female body, the homosexual male must never live vicariously through the heterosexual female, or any female for that matter, and must never live vicariously as if he were a heterosexual female. To do otherwise is inherently self-defeating. In addition, the homosexual male must understand that the heterosexual female, because of her biology, is not and can never be a *fellow traveler*; rather, the homosexual male must understand that the heterosexual female, in relation to the homosexual male, is always an *agent provocateur*, regardless whether she knows it or not and/or regardless whether she wants to be or not.

8. Last, but most importantly, upon absorbing and applying all of the above, the homosexual male must permanently live *the mathematical equation that is masculinity*. Because of Heterosexual Supremacy, which propagates The Heterosexual Manifesto, most homosexual male's sense of *self-worth* is all but nonexistent, so 99.9% of homosexual males suffer from extreme neurosis. This extreme neurosis is the source of all self-defeating behavior on the part of the homosexual male (primarily exemplified by the escapist, self-delusional action of living vicariously through the heterosexual female or living vicariously as if he were a heterosexual female). To overcome this extreme neurosis, separate from currently configured civilization, and live *the mathematical equation that is masculinity*, the homosexual male must first become *self-actualized*. Self-actualization can only be achieved by becoming neurosis-free, and this is possible by applying the principles set forth in Dr. Wayne W. Dyer's masterpiece *The Sky's The Limit*.

Axiom 12

Without fear of seeming redundant, and for clarity's sake: because the female has no *sexual biomechanical requirement*, the female, regardless of sexual orientation, is notionally irrelevant and wholly dependent on the exclusive heterosexual male for procreation; therefore, the lesbian, unfortunately, by her mere female biology, however unbeknownst, unwilling, or unwitting, is axiomatically a part of Heterosexual Supremacy, resulting in The Heterosexual Manifesto. (See Axiom 1 and Axiom 4.) (Because the female is notionally irrelevant, lesbianism is a problem for heterosexual supremacist only because male homosexuality exist; if male homosexuality did not exist, heterosexual supremacist would have no problem with lesbianism—as evidenced by the fact that whenever there is a complete absence of male homosexuality, lesbianism is considered either erotic and/or quaint by heterosexists. *Quod Erat Demonstrandum.*) It understood that lesbianism is a part of Heterosexual Supremacy that inevitably leads to The Heterosexual Manifesto, the homosexual male must come to terms with the fact, because of the *sui generis* nature of male homosexuality, juxtaposed to the mediocrity of female homosexuality, that the lesbian and the homosexual male have irreconcilable sexual, social and political goals—the homosexual male must then take the extraordinarily radical step of having absolutely nothing to do with lesbians (and/or their supposed liberation), let alone having anything to do with straight females (and/or their supposed liberation)! In short, the homosexual male should have absolutely nothing to do with all females, whether they are straight or lesbian, however agonizing this may be for the homosexual male and/or females. Some may label this as so-called separatist, but labels are made to be ignored.

Précis

Dedicated To Jean-Paul Sartre For Writing
Being And Nothingness: An Essay On Phenomenological Ontology

Testosterone: A World Without Faggots

All I have in this world is my balls and my word, and I don't break them for no one.

—Tony Montana from the movie Scareface
(as if you didn't already now).

If there is a God, he, she, or it has providently placed the homosexual male in a *sui generis* concurrence: a life immediately threatened simply by virtue of having been born. For lack of a better description, the homosexual male is born completely and totally alone in a forest of mirrors—there is no fairy godmother to nourish and nurture him, there is no fairy godfather to protect and provide for him—and he must find his way out of this forest of mirrors, all on his own, or he will wither and die. (For even greater clarity of the homosexual male's predicament, reference the *Myth Of Narcissus.*) The extraordinarily *sui generis* birth of the homosexual male, and the extreme hardship therein, is not a judgment of God, if there is a God, any more than the birth of someone into royalty is a judgment of God; it is simply the luck of the draw. Get over it and get on with it.

Because effeminacy in a male (the male body) is unquestionably 100% useless and thus axiomatically self-defeating—remember, femininity is only "tolerated" in the sole context of the female body, and only "tolerated" in the sole context of the female body because the female body is absolutely necessary for procreation—*sexual realpolitik* dictates that the homosexual male only has one or two choices: 1.) sex reassignment surgery or 2.) man up! I don't mean to be flippant or mean to be mean, but I really don't know how else to put it. (And I am supposed to be a wordsmith!) It's not that I am necessarily at a loss for words, but that words really are not adequate to describe the utter lack of choices that *sexual realpolitik* provide the homosexual male—but then, nobody ever said life was fair (see Axiom 1).

The Mathematical Equation That Is Masculinity

Contrary to popular mythology, some people aren't simply born *masculine* and other people simply born *feminine*; in other words, masculinity, like femininity, is not some ethereal, ephemeral thing that cannot be quantified and qualified. Masculinity, like femininity, is an actual physical thing that can be seen, heard, tasted, smelled, and touched. The difference between *the physical-physicality of masculinity* and *the physical-physicality of femininity*, is that the *physical-physicality of masculinity* is never a given and must always be earned, while the *physical-physicality of femininity* is always a given and never needs to be earned—all a female has to do is "grow" breasts and she is a female, but **a male cannot simply "grow" a body like the one on the jacket-cover of this book; a body like the one on the jacket-cover of this book must always, always be earned!** Thus, the *physical-physicality of masculinity* has value, but the *physical-physicality of femininity* is valueless. (Obviously, anything that must be earned, axiomatically, has "value" and anything that does not need to be earned, axiomatically, is "valueless.") Understanding that the *physical-physicality of masculinity* must always be earned and that *physical-physicality of femininity* never needs to be earned is essential to understanding *the mathematical equation that is masculinity*.

The other thing to understand about *the physical-physicality of masculinity* is that it has a value "behavioral" component, not just a value physical component, that wholly distinguishes it from the valueless "behavioral" component of femininity; and this is the reason why there is so much misunderstanding, consternation, and obsession over what exactly is and what exactly isn't masculinity and, more importantly, who does and who doesn't have masculinity, who is and who isn't masculine. (In example, a man may have a physically masculine body like the one on the jacket-cover of this book, but where he to exhibit effeminate or cowardly "behavior" it would literally and figuratively negate his physically masculine body and literally and figuratively render his physically masculine body mute or nonexistent.) What, exactly, is this ineffable "behavioral" component of masculinity that has such incalculable value? The behavioral component of masculinity that has such inestimable value is, in one simple word, *stoicism*. But all of this is academic, as Camille Paglia will gladly tell you. Because the mathematical equation that is masculinity is one part masculine body and the other part masculine behavior (*stoicism*), it goes without saying that tailoring both your body and your behavior will result in masculinity.

(Is Valueless)
Feminine Body And/Or Feminine Behavior =
The Physical-Physicality Of Femininity

(Never Needs To Be Earned)
Feminine Body And/Or Feminine Behavior = Femininity = Weakness

(Is Neither The Means Nor The End)
Weakness = Femininity = Feminine Body And/Or Feminine Behavior

(Is Valuable)
Masculine Body + Masculine Behavior =
The Physical-Physicality Of Masculinity

(Always Must Be Earned)
Masculine Body + Masculine Behavior = Masculinity = Strength

(Is Both The Means & The End)
Strength = Masculinity = Masculine Body + Masculine Behavior

Unlike femininity, because masculinity requires an alchemic symbiosis of masculine body *and* masculine behavior that must always be earned, you cannot have one part of the masculine equation without the other part of the masculine equation. In other words, for masculinity to exist, you cannot have masculine body without masculine behavior, you cannot have masculine behavior without masculine body; they are interdependent and wholly inseparable, and one without the other is always *faute de mieux*. (Femininity, however, exist whether you have feminine body or feminine behavior separately, it is not required that you have both feminine body and feminine behavior together for femininity to exist; and, remember, neither feminine body nor feminine behavior must be earned.) In other words, unlike femininity, masculinity can only be achieved by way of masculinity; it is both the means and the end, the alpha and the omega. And therein lies the rub—you must already have masculinity in order to earn masculinity, you must already be masculine to be masculine; the same way you can't get a job unless you have experience, but how do you get experience if you can't get a job. (Although no one is so-called "born masculine" or is so-called "naturally" masculine, it should be understood that some people are born with a *masculine genetic predisposition* and/or a *masculine environment predisposition* that gives them, how can I put it gently, something of a masculine head start or leg up. Like all of life, the environment you are born into and raised in and the genetics you are born with, are the luck of the draw. Entropy rears its ugly head once again.) It would seem the quest to achieve and insure masculinity in every male is the ultimate in "chasing the dragon."

Although you now know what exactly masculinity is, because "how" to actually achieve masculinity (masculine body and masculine behavior)—that is, if you don't already have it—has literally stumped countless others, I will not fall into the trap of telling you it is even possible to achieve masculinity; probable, perhaps, but possible depends on a host of factors beyond both my and your control. That said, having detailed *the mathematical equation that is masculinity*, explaining the task of "how" to achieve the perfect alchemy of masculine body and masculine behavior requires a book all its own. I am sure you wait with bated breath.

Conclusion:

**Dedicated To Crusading, Muckraking Journalist I.F. Stone
For Writing *The Trial Of Socrates* And For Being Izzy Stone**

For the sole purpose of being redundant: one man's Utopia is another man's Dystopia. That understood, the fact that we all live in an Orwellian heterosexual fascist state may be relative, but you can rest assured that the world would probably be in an even sadder and pathetic state if we all lived in an Orwellian homosexual fascist state—were such a thing even possible, of course. What's the alternative to *sexual fascism*, of any kind, you ask. Well, it's *sexual anarchy* as far as the eye can see, that's what sexual fascists, cloaked as conservatives, quickly interject. Look, I don't pretend to have any, let alone all, of the answers here, but *political correctness* on the right, left, and center only exacerbates an already mind-boggling problem. The only thing I know is that I think I know that I think I know this: 1.) because *Heterosexual Supremacy* exist, the homosexual male (and only the homosexual male) is *sui generis persona non grata ad infinitum* and therefore he has *irreconcilable differences* with all of currently configured civilization (*The Heterosexual Manifesto*), and he can never be properly accepted and integrated into the sexual pantheon; 2.) the homosexual male, who is clearly in denial (and the lesbian, who is clearly in even more denial), is simply going to have to face up to the indisputable fact that, because *Heterosexual Supremacy* exist, he, the homosexual male is *sui generis persona non grata ad infinitum*; 3.) and then, the homosexual male (without any assist from the lesbian, because it isn't going to come) must take the appropriate actions, however agonizing and seemingly antisocial, to seek an amicable divorce from currently configured civilization (*The Heterosexual Manifesto*). And with that, I bid you adieu.

Answer To My Critics:

Ban This Book!

Or, For Christ's Sake, Be Kind Enough To At Least Get In A Huff

Dedicated To Giordana Bruno
Ex-Dominican Monk Burned At The Stake By Pope Clemente VIII
For Believing In Science Not Voodoo

We can easily forgive a child who is afraid of the dark; the real tragedy of life is when men are afraid of the light.

—Plato

If you think everything that I have written in this work is nonsensical bullshit, not to mention extremely dangerous, you are absolutely right. I wrote this book to purposely *incite* you, and all and sundry, to *non-violently* question everything that you hold sacred and dear (including dear ole' mom and dad); and, I wrote it to, hopefully, *incite* you to bring about a *Sexual Velvet Revolution*. And it is precisely because of my dispassionate literary, philosophical, and free-thinking hijinks that this work is, technically, obscene and thus, theoretically, illegal. So, you should get busy on banning this book!

Don't forget that everybody, including yourself, has only his own experience to think with.

—Rudolf Flesch

Addendum Parting Shot

Dedicated to Legendary Mathematician Alan Turing
For Inventing The Turing Machine, For Being A Fag, And For Being A Logician

---

Frailty, thy name is woman!
—Shakespeare's Hamlet

If the homosexual male, who is in a *sui generis* position of sexual and social disenfranchisement, does not have the mental, emotional and physical wherewithal to make a clean and full break from currently configured civilization (*The Heterosexual Manifesto*), the homosexual male must have the strength, perseverance, and balls to radically change (problem prevent and problem solve) currently configured civilization:

1. He must invent an alternative womb.

   — Heterosexists, fascists, and theocrats, cloaked as so-called conservatives and/or as so-called ethicists, will howl that you are "playing God" and will outlaw the invention of the alternative womb; since the monopoly of the female womb to gestate, incubate, and birth children is the fount from which all *Heterosexual Supremacy* springs.

2. He must find the cure for and the vaccine for *all* venereal and sexually transmitted diseases.

   — Heterosexists, fascists, and theocrats, cloaked as so-called conservatives and/or as so-called ethicists, will surreptitiously do everything in their power to prevent humanity from ever finding the cure and finding the vaccine for all venereal and sexually transmitted diseases; since venereal and sexually transmitted diseases are foundational to the Voodoo that they use to terrorize humanity into heterosexism.

All the Machiavellian, conniving, and underhanded attempts by cryptoheterosexists, cryptofascists, and cryptotheocrats to outlaw the invention of the alternative womb and all the diabolical, devious, and oblique attempts by cryptoheterosexists, cryptofascists, and cryptotheocrats to clandestinely stymie finding the cure and finding the vaccine for all venereal and sexually transmitted diseases will be for naught—change is the only constant; the only question is will there be change for the better or will there be change for the worse. Because of the *sui generis* sexual and social disfranchisement of the homosexual male, and only the homosexual male—which is *The Heterosexual Manifesto*, that results from *Heterosexual Surpremacy*—the homosexual male, for his own survival, must never let others define for him what "better" and what "worse" mean!

An Especially Pyrrhonic Note To So-Called Feminists

Dedicated To The Ancient Great Lyric Poet Sapphos, Born On The Isle Of Lesbos

The object of education lies not in communicating the values of the past, but in creating new values of the future.

—John Dewey

The fact is irrefutable that we currently live in a totalitarian heterosexist police state that is purposely and solely designed to break the will, soul and spirit of the homosexual male—and only the homosexual male. It is also irrefutable fact that this sad state of affairs, heretofore christened *The Heterosexual Manifesto*, is the direct result of the self-loathing and masochism of the female (and, by extension, the self-loathing and masochism of the effeminate homosexual male). Having pointed all this out, I will hear shrieks of misogynist (and hate speech monger) hurled at me by all and sundry, but particularly by females, and some males, who profess to be so-called feminist. Well, talk about the pot calling the kettle black! The female sense of self-loathing and masochism literally knows no bounds and they are hell bent on having company for their self-inflicted misery. Pointing this out to them, it would seem, is all the more justification for their self-loathing and masochism. (If females were so proud of being females they wouldn't be so threatened by competition—i.e. the alternative womb etc.) But all this is academic. How many times can I point out that life is unspeakably unfair and that females got the short end of stick? The problem is that females exacerbate an already bad situation by not doing the extremely hard work necessary to not exacerbate the entropy of life and the universe. (Entropy is essentially where all of life's "unfairness"—at least as far as we human beings understand "unfairness"—springs.) With all due respect to the great Helen Reddy (whose music and voice I adore), females need to man up, then put up, or shut up! Enduring the pain of child birth is not enough; **the female must endure the pain of never having to endure the pain of child birth—because, in the future, which will have an alternative womb, child birthing by females will be considered barbaric and downright torture for both mother and child.** Scary having to give up the one tool in your tool box, isn't it, females? Well, resistance is futile.

Females, your desire to hold onto your sexual monopoly is telling. And you're probably none too happy I found your weak spot by way of critique. (And will most likely do everything you can to shut me up so no one else finds out about your weak spot.) Well, which is it going to be, so-called feminists? Are you a human being who insist on being treated as an absolute equal human being capable of error or are you a sacred cow who insist on being worshipped like an infallible deity? You can't have it both ways. Your insistence on having your cake and eating it too is the ultimate refutation of your claimed desire to be treated as an equal. If you are an equal, you are open to dissection and criticism just like everybody else; if you are not open to dissection and criticism like everyone else, then you certainly and inherently are not a so-called "equal," since no one group or person is beyond reproach. If I have said it once I have said it a thousand times: there are no sacred cows! (And the lest of all sacred cows are LGBT folk, who, in this withering tract, come away even more scathed than females.) Enough with your insistence that girls be treated as equally as boys, so long as girls get treated "special." (Notice I didn't say get treated with "kid gloves," I said get treated "special.") Feminism is a double-edged sword, you see. Which end of the sword will you cut your own throat with?

Females: your sexual monopoly on child birth will eventually come to an end and then you will be forced to deal with the consequences of not having done the extremely hard work to make yourself something other than a vassal for human procreation; your net worth and value will be less than zero because you were lazy and insisted that God had your back (not understanding that the only constant is CHANGE and therefore CHANGE is God); you will be found out, and then discarded and dismissed, for the blackmailer of humanity that you are.

I personally won't be around to say "I told you so," but this trailblazing, pioneering, experimental, and mind-bogglingly dialectical treatise, *The Heterosexual Manifesto*, will act in my stead.

So let it be written, so let it be done.

Dénouement

Dedicated To Benedictus de Spinoza, One Of The All Time Great Thinkers

Let's admit the case of the conservative: if we once start thinking, no one can guarantee where we shall come out; except that many ends, objects and institutions are doomed. Every thinker puts some portion of an apparently stable world in peril, and no one can wholly predict what will emerge in its place.

—John Dewey

The *Philanthrope?*

God: You are the mythological Narcissus!

Homo Sapien: Oh, no, am I not doomed to wither?!

God: To save humanity from itself;
      You must destroy Heterosexual Supremacy!

Homo Sapien: But how, God?! How?!

God: Remember, the world is a Plutocracy!
      There is no problem so big
      That a little money can't solve

Homo Sapien: But I don't understand, God!

God: Just know this
    Change is the only constant
    And money changes everything

The Misanthrope?

I prophesize that
I am not a prophet
And
Because I have prophesized I am not a prophet
I *do not* prophesize that
Heterosexuality only breeds compulsory heterosexuality
And that
Compulsory heterosexuality only breeds religious fascism
And that
Religious fascism will be Womankind's and Mankind's undoing
And
Because I have prophesized I am not a prophet
I *do not* prophesize that
My prophecy that I am not a prophet
Will be proven right
Or wrong

www.ingramcontent.com/pod-product-compliance
Lightning Source LLC
Chambersburg PA
CBHW021246280526
45784CB00005B/2252